Daddy, You Have Told This Before

Dr. Bernard Bull
Professor Emeritus
Carson Newman College

Daddy, You Have Told This Before

Dr. Bernard Bull
Professor Emeritus
Carson Newman College

Mossy Creek Press

Daddy, You've Told This Before.

ISBN: Softcover 978-1-949888-29-4

Copyright © 2012 by Bernard Bull

All rights reserved. No part of this book may be reproduced or transmitted in any form or by any means, electronic or mechanical, including photocopying, recording, or by any information storage and retrieval system, without permission in writing from the publisher.

To order additional copies of this book, contact:

Mossy Creek Press

1-423-475-7308

www.mossycreekpress.com

Mossy Creek Press is an imprint of Parson's Porch & Company (PP&C) in Cleveland, Tennessee. PP&C is an innovative non-profit organization which raises money by publishing books of noted authors, representing all genres. All profits are shared with Carson-Newman College for student scholarships.

Table of Contents

Acknowledgements   7

Introduction   9

The Early Years: New Zion and Etowah   11

Student Days at Carson Newman College   53

The Early Years with Barbara   59

The Years on Carson Newman Faculty   97

Mission Trips   155

The Grandchildren   167

The Promise   179

The Conclusion and Post Script   183

Acknowledgements

My mom's memoir was titled, "The Glory is Not Mine." She was widowed at a young age with eight sons and pregnant with me. We moved from a dairy farm in Bradley County to a tenant house (shack) on my adoptive grandfather's farm in New Zion Community of McMinn County. Years later, Mom looked back with thanksgiving to God for the blessings we had received.

From that Lincoln log cabin idea of my beginning I was able to finish college and three graduate degrees and spend 37 years educating college students to become teachers and in later years I was able to travel on several international trips including, Russia, China, and South Africa. Therefore, I acknowledge God's grace, my mother's love, my brothers' fellowship, my teachers' discipline and teaching and most importantly my wife who has been a perfect help mate for me. We have three of the best children who ever lived:

Dr. Bradley Wayne Bull, married to Dr. Connie Lynne Cruze Bull; Benita Elizabeth Bull Claiborne, married to Daniel Heath Claiborne; Bethany Lyn Bull Carpenter, married to Keith Allen Carpenter.

I honor my children's spouses as my own children. All three proposals of marriage were made at our house. Connie's parents were at our dining room table when Bradley proposed to Connie. Both suitors of our daughters came to our house to ask permission to marry our daughters. They have all heard my stories, sometimes more than once!

If you are reading this book, I acknowledge you and hope you enjoy and learn as your read. You may reach me at bbull@cn.edu.

Introduction

"Daddy, You've Told This Before."

If you have offspring and live long enough, you will hear them say, "Daddy, you've told that story before...a thousand times. I could even tell it for you and not miss a word." As the number of children increases the repetition multiplies because you forget to whom the story has been told. Well, you don't want anyone to feel left out of the fun, so you retell it any way, while they plan for your time in a nursing home.

The Early Years: New Zion and Etowah

The Coming of Electricity

My mother's uncle and aunt adopted her after her parents died. Everyone in the community called mom's adopted father, Uncle Taylor. I just called him Paw. We were standing under a cedar tree on his 47 acre farm when two men from the electricity company came to see him. They explained to him that they were running electric lines up through the community and they needed to go through his farm. His reply to them was, "If God had wanted electricity through here He would have already had the poles up." The two men reasoned with Paw that people up

the valley wanted electricity and they could not proceed unless they could put at least one pole on his farm. Being a Godly man, and a

good neighbor he agreed to ONE pole if they would put it as far behind the barn as possible. That is where they put it. Paw continued to crank his record player with the record being very thick and music on only one side. He also continued to wind his seven day Grandfather clock that sat on the mantle above the fire place.

About 60 years later my oldest brother allowed me to purchase 3 acres of the land that included the spring. We cleaned the property and built a small cabin. We put up one electric pole and that is what is still there today.

Dam at the Spring and Need for Prayer

After Dad died, we moved to New Zion community in McMinn County, six miles west of Etowah. We lived in a small wood shack on Uncle Taylor's farm. It was a tarpaper sided house. By this time only seven of the boys were living at home. Uncle Taylor had a spring and spring house where Aunt Hattie kept her milk and eggs. The branch from the spring ran through the back field of the part of the farm on which we lived. I was about 3 years old when the house caught fire. I remember the older boys running back and forth to the spring to carry buckets of water to throw on the burning wall behind the warm-morning stove. I sat and watched. Thinking back I wonder why they did not at least take me outside but it may have been too cold for that.

In the summer we boys used rocks and mud to make a dam in the branch so we could go skinny dipping during the hot day. We built such a good dam that we had a place to swim. Unbeknown to us the dam was so good that the water backed up into Grandma Watson's (Aunt Hattie) spring and turned over her milk crock. She came down the path toward our dam with a big stick and in a matter of seconds destroyed our day's work and our week of fun. She also had some harsh words with Mom about, "Makin them youngins behave." She didn't cuss but it was only because she didn't know any cuss words.

The best of families have conflicts but we learned to work through the conflicts and love one another. Ms B and I built a cabin there. It has a sign; "Uncle Taylor's Cabin,

Aunt Hattie's Spring". Aunt Hattie (grandmaw) protected that spring like it was gold and she tied her change in the corner of a handkerchief. Money was tight.

I rode to New Zion Baptist Church with Grandpa Watson (Uncle Taylor) in his horse drawn buggy. It was at that church in the front yard, under the big oak tree that I first learned what prayer was. At about age 4, I sat on a root of that tree one evening with the men who prayed. The women went up to the cemetery to pray.

When I was almost 6 years old we moved to Etowah. The two older brothers, Hoyt and Eldon, had gone off to World War II. They sent money home so Mom could get a house in town. Often I heard her on her knees, praying out loud for her military sons. Years later when I visited Pearl Harbor and went on the memorial, I was glad to see not one Bull name on the list of those who gave their lives in the Japanese attack.

Stolen Cookies are Sweet

This is the story which led my son to think I was normal,...well, not as saintly as he had thought.

The man who drove the "Rolling Store" took his sales brochure into the house to try to sell his wares to my mom. He left the sliding door to the truck open and I went into the "store" and there on the dash was a box of Fig Newton cookies. I was 6, maybe 7 years old and could use the excuse that I was hungry and much tempted. I was too inexperienced as a thief or not greedy enough to take the whole box so I opened it and took only 2 or 3.

When the man returned to the truck and saw the opened box he immediately went back into the house to tell my mom. She

bought the box of Fig Newton cookies. It may have been her last dime but I'm sure she did not want her boy to go to jail over two cookies, or the family to be disgraced at having a thief. I have a foggy memory of what happened next but I try to imagine that she made me eat the whole box. I do not recall any punishment for the incident. Maybe I cried so much she felt sorry for me. Do I still love Fig Newton cookies? Yes, I purchase them often and they serve as a reminder to my children that as a child I also was "NORMAL". That is why I created my own tee shirt that says, "We each has flaus." This points to Romans 3:23 in the Bible.

Left in Harriman

Being the "baby" (translation youngest) of nine sons was often a challenge. The older brothers did have a reputation and I was following in their footsteps but it was easy to get lost in the crowd. Never was that more obvious than when we went on a short trip with my brother Russell who owned an exterminating company. There was a car full of us who went to Harriman, Tennessee to visit one of Russell's businesses. We stopped down town to get something to eat. Near the end of our time there I went to the restroom. When I came back the place was empty. I assume they paid the bill. I was in a strange town with not a penny to my name and knew no one there. I walked out on the sidewalk

and just stood there wondering what I should do. While I waited, the car, still full of brothers, was riding around enjoying the fellowship. They happened to drive back by our eating place and fortunately one of them said, "There's Bernard". They stopped and picked me up. Amazingly, they had not missed me. No wonder I have psychological fears of being left alone.

The Watermelon and the Wagon Ride

From down town Etowah to my house was about a mile up Eighth Street to Scott Avenue. Streets were numerals and avenues were mostly names of states. Tennessee Avenue was down town and the second one was Ohio. On the corner of Eight Street and Ohio Avenue there was a vacant lot where the farmers sold produce.

I was about eight or nine years old and had started walking up Eighth toward home. I had thoughts sometimes wondering what my dad was like since he had died in February before I was born in August. I wondered what kind of man my dad might have been. I had only one or two photographs of him. I did not know the word "contemplation" but that was what I was doing or praying. I was concerned but knew no one to ask.

At the corner of Ohio and Eighth I stopped to look at the watermelon knowing that I had no money with which to purchase even a slice. A farmer asked who I was and I told him my name. His response was, "You're Rufus's boy, ain't ye? "Yes, I am." He picked up a very large watermelon and broke it on the sidewalk, looked at me and said, "Eat the heart where there are no seeds." The heart of that watermelon was huge and sweet but the knowledge that here was a man who loved my dad so much that he would give to me the heart of the biggest melon was much sweeter.

On another day I was walking up Eighth Street toward home when I heard the sound of a horse drawn wagon behind me. I looked around and the man asked if I wanted a ride up the hill. I sure did because it was getting steep. I climbed up on the wagon beside the man. The conversation went immediately to my identity upon which he asked if I was the son of Rufus. I assured him that I was and he proceeded to tell me that he used to be "bad to drink." (That was a euphemism for alcoholic or drunk.) He said that my dad had talked him into being sober and he was indeed still sober and selling milk, eggs and other farm products.

I'm sure my dad was not perfect but I know he was a positive influence on a number of people including that he probably had greater influence on me than on any other person. As he lay dying at the dairy farm in Bradley County he told my Mom, "Be sure the boys get a good education." After hearing my Mom tell that story, I took it as a personal challenge to complete college which was more than any of the eight brothers ahead of me had done. I also had a calling to be what God wanted me to be.

The Year of NO CHRISTMAS PRESENT

Although the Bull family was blessed in many ways, we did not have much money. Christmas did not mean that we would get toys. We might get a gift basket from a church or civic group. Sometimes we got several baskets. We ate well at Christmas. The first toy that I remember was a xylophone. It had eight keys of different colors. I suppose I was expected to play the eight pieces of colored tin with the wood hammer.

As the older brothers got married and had jobs they began to buy presents for the younger brothers who still lived at home. They brought all their families to our house for Christmas. Mom opened her presents last and she was always so blessed and thankful.

But she always handed out the gifts to everyone else first. The gifts were under the real cedar or pine tree that we got from the forest. One year as we sat there with Mom handing out the gifts I watched in amazement as everyone filled the floor with wrapping paper except me. I received nothing. Not even a piece of stick candy. I was very sad. The trickster, Marcel, had his usual grin that came on when he was up to something. After he saw me sweat for a few minutes he took me to the back bedroom and looked under the bed. There were all of my presents that he had hidden.

As an adult I learned that it is more blessed to give than to receive. When I have assisted with delivering a Christmas basket to a needy family I remember being a receiver of such generosity.

Taking food to a family in my car is better than sitting in a house waiting to see if someone is bringing food to me. I know what it is to not get a toy for Christmas. I know more now what a joy it is to give a toy. Next Christmas ask someone,

"What was the favorite thing you **gave** this Christmas.?"

The Nail

Three blocks from my house and just across the street from the current Etowah Grammar School, there lived a family by the name of Householder. When I was big enough to push a roller blade lawn mower Mr. Householder would let me make a little money mowing his yard. Thankfully it was a level yard. Those roller blades could easily get bounded up in high grass. The yard was separated from the garden by a concrete block wall that was about 3 feet tall and uncapped. One day Mr. Householder found a nail and as he handed it to me he said, "Put this somewhere that it will never be a problem of getting into a tire." I thought a few seconds and walked over to the concrete block wall and dropped the nail into an open block. He told me that I had made a good choice.

He went inside the house and returned with a book in his hand which he handed to me. At the time I did not own a single book. This book would become a prized possession because it was commonly called a "Blue Backed Speller". Years latter when I was working in Teacher Education as a Language Arts teacher I would use the Noah Webster spelling book. It remains a treasure to me and I got it as a boy because I was smart enough to know how to get rid of a nail. Maybe Mr. Householder saw in me something that I had not yet seen in myself: A future teacher who would need books.

Split the Toe

It was, in retrospect, a dumb game but often played by boys who had learned, or in this case, were learning, to throw a knife and stick it in the ground or log, or something. Some boys had the double bladed knives with the big and small blades. Wow, you had an extra chance to make it stick! The game we played was called Split. The players stood facing each other about three feet apart. Each had his feet tightly together. One player threw a knife NEAR the other's foot and he moved his foot out to the knife IF the knife was stuck in the ground. Then the other player threw his knife NEAR the other player. This game continued until one was split out so far that he fell down. The one to fall was the one who lost. This game would normally be played with shoes on. However, on this day a neighbor boy, Edward Bates and I were barefoot. Edward had seven sisters and I had eight brothers; no wonder he spent more time at our house than at his. It was half a block across a backyard from our house to his. Edward was three years my senior and should have had better brains than to play the game with me and especially to let me throw first. This game ended abruptly when my first throw stuck the short blade into his little toe. He pulled the knife out and ran, hopped, limped across the backyards leaving little blood samples along the way.

Shortly our phone rang and I answered it. Mrs. Bates wanted urgently to speak to Bernard. I handed the phone to my brother Jimmy and stood there watching him get the chewing out of his life. Fortunately our mom was not home at this time. That saved us both from punishment and Jimmy saved me from a chewing out. What are big brothers for any way?

The rest of the story: Edward has had TWO heart transplants and gives his age as the average of the hearts he has received. Maybe I prepared him for experiencing the knife!

Pickles and Pepsis

It was great fun when we had soft drinks to put salt into the bottle and shake it like crazy and spew the fizz into our mouth or on a nearby brother. On this particular hot summer day mom was in the kitchen chopping up cucumbers for making pickles. She used a rather large butcher knife.

On that day we had somehow gotten two or three Pepsi Colas and started the salt, shake and spew fun. Mom yelled for us to "Stop it". Mom NEVER repeated her commands. Normally we minded what we heard the first time but today the salt was already in the bottle. Anyhow, Linford missed the command altogether and spewed it into his mouth and received immediate judgment from above by becoming chocked. As he gasped for breath, brother Tony, wanting to be helpful, did what was recommended before the Heimlich Maneuver was invented, and slapped Linford hard on the back. The hit propelled him through the kitchen and behind Mom. She turned quickly and swatted Linford on the butt with the butcher knife. Thankfully she was nimble enough to turn the knife so that it contacted his butt with a FLAT swat; otherwise we would have been in surgery on a rump roast. Bull that is!

Halloween

Halloween was one night when our mom let the five boys still living at home go out on the town of Etowah to trick or treat. It was a safe town so we had no curfew. It was a cold night and I had worn a heavy coat. At one house I threw a rock at a large plate glass window. Then I ran as fast as I could right into a wire attached to two trees. The wire hit on my chest and my feet went flying into the night sky. The only damage except ego was the red strip across my chest. Later I heard the man of the house say to some other trick-or-treaters, "My baby was sleeping in the bassinet just under that window. Had the glass broken, no telling what damage could have been done." If my mom had known what I did that night, no telling what damage would have been done and it would not have been on my chest. This event took place one block down the street from Mrs. Graham who lived on 8th Street.

Mr. Graham worked out of town most of the time and also he died rather young I think. Anyway, I never knew him. Mrs. Graham however was like an angel on Halloween night. Most children wanted to go to her door to get a treat and no one would ever think of tricking her. However, my brothers and I were invited into her house and right to the kitchen table. She had that melt in your mouth white divinity fudge, chocolate fudge and several other sweets with nuts in them. All homemade! No store bought stuff.

Mrs. Graham made no restrictions on how much we could eat while drinking our hot chocolate. And there was some to take home.

It is now sad to pass the old home place and see it so run down after her passing, but the memory of Mrs. Graham and her kindness will never pass.

Out All Night

Being the early riser I have always been, I was on the front porch watching the sun come up over Star Mountain. I was eight years old. Out the street I saw my brother Marcel coming with a slow walk. He gave a sign for me to be very quiet. He slipped the door open and entered the room, quietly took off his shoes and got in bed. Just as his head hit the pillow Mom said, "Marcel, I need you in the kitchen". By the time she finished the sentence she was standing beside the bed, waiting for movement in her direction. He moved and followed her to the kitchen. She needed him in the kitchen the entire day. He was not out of her sight. That evening, whatever plans he had previously made were abolished because he was exhausted. He went to bed really early. He was 18 and still had to mind his Mom.

Several years later, when he had three grown boys, he pruned Mom's Grab Apple tree without her permission. She did not want the tree pruned and took one of the limbs and whipped him with it. We never got too old to mind our Mom. Maybe that is why she was nominated to be Tennessee Mother of the Year. I wish we had more parents today who knew how to make their children mind.

The Clothes Pins

During high school I worked for a family who owned a hardware/furniture store. The wife needed help around the house and that is where I had my first experience with painting. It was a concrete back patio. Later I got a real job at the store down town.

At the hardware store there was a big wash tub on rollers that was filled with clothes pins. The sign on the tub simply said, 10 cents. We would roll the tub out to the sidewalk at the store entrance. One day a man told me that he wanted a dozen of the wooden clothes pins. I put the pins in a paper bag and went to the cash register in the back of the store and told him it would be a dollar and twenty cents. The owner, sitting in his office, heard me

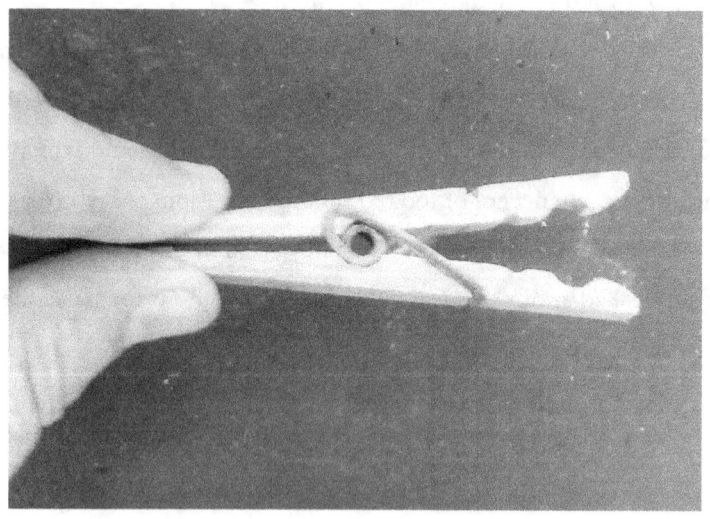

and stuck his head out the door to say, "The clothes pins are 10 cents a dozen". I took the man's dime and he left. Then the boss came out, looked at me and said, "I'd make a lot more money if I did it your way."

Fifty-five years later, which was this month, I saw some wooden clothes pins in a store and my pricing was about 60 years ahead of its time. Most children today only see plastic clothes pins. They also would not know what a Louisville Slugger is. That is a baseball bat, made of WOOD.

The One Legged Girl

She came to town and became an instant hit. Thinking of her reminds me of the joke about the girl who was pregnant out of wedlock and her father said he would kill the guilty party. Someone told him, "We have narrowed it down to two. It was either the football team or the basketball team." This girl was that notorious for group events. At a local service station she reportedly would go up in a car on the grease rack and have sex. When the car was brought back down another guy would get in, go up and come down. In one night the car could go up and down several times. She is famed for kicking a guy out of a car with her half leg. (Her leg was amputated at the knee.) He landed on the ground outside the car. Thankfully, for him, it was not on the grease rack. I suspect that I heard these stories from my older brothers and I have no idea that they ever participated in these events.

This notorious whore lived only a block and a half from our house which was at the end of the road. The city limit ran through our back yard and Scott Avenue ended at our yard. I was 12 or 13 at the time and played Little League baseball. I could cross a cow pasture and go cross country through the woods to the ball field rather than walk the half mile via the streets.

One day the one legged girl called our house. (I just stopped to wonder, how in the world did she know our number? Maybe she looked it up by our name and she was desperate. I'll ask brother the next time I see him.) It was a rare time indeed that

I was home alone. She said she wanted to come to the house to visit me. Hanging up the phone I went to the edge of the yard and looked down Scott Avenue and sure enough there was the woman on crutches, hobbling toward my house. I grabbed a baseball glove and disappeared into the woods toward the baseball field which was two blocks as the crow flies. The street route would have gone by her house. I don't know how disappointed she was when she arrived at an empty house. Had I been 16, 17, 18, this story may have had a tragic ending. As it is, it is just a memory of being pursued by an older, desperate woman.

It would be some years before I started to read the book of Proverbs and learn about evil women lurking for naïve men.

Canada Dry and Cookies

Our scout leader was a local attorney. He took us places but left most of the work up to the leadership of the troop officers. We were on a trip to the camp ground on the Hiwassee River. For some reason I had been able to purchase a large bottle of Ginger Ale. All our cooking was to be over an open fire and a cool drink would be really good. However, we had no coolers or ice. The coolest thing around was the running water of the river. I found a place beside the bank where I could submerge my bottle of Ginger Ale where it would not float away. By the time the evening meal was cooked my drink would be cold.

Later that day I went down to the river and retrieved my bottle, popped the cap and turned it up to take a large gulp. Looking up through the green bottle in the sun light I saw small leaves and grass! Some of the older boys had enjoyed drinking my Ginger Ale and refilled the bottle with river water and put the cap back on. Typical child abuse!

At the end of the eighth grade the room mothers were treating us to a trip to Lake Winnepesaukah, in Chattanooga. It the 1950's that was the nearest thing we had to Disney World. There were rides all over the place and my favorite was the trip through the dark tunnel, up the ramp and down the roller coaster ride. We could hold a girl's hand during this ride. Wow!.

Then the room mothers had a picnic for us. There was plenty of food. In fact they had some left over. One of the mothers gave to me a whole, unopened, box of cookies. I took the box home and put it in my drawer. I say drawer because we boys did not have a room. We shared a room with brothers. But I did have a personal drawer; though not private as you will see.

The next afternoon I came home from somewhere to see two brothers sitting on the front door steps. Smiling and rubbing crumbs off their faces. They ate my whole box of cookies. Typical younger brother abuse! I guess they paid me back for stealing the Fig Newton's before I was in first grade. The wheels of justice grind slowly but exceeding fine.

My Left Handed Brother

As children and youth brothers whose ages are close seem to get along less than those separated by some years. Two of my brothers did not really get along well. They fought often. It is called sibling rivalry. I didn't know that then, I just thought they hated each other. My favorite brother was 10 years my senior. No sibling rivalry there. These two brothers who hated each other continued their rivalry into high school. I'll call them A and J with A being the older.

One day at school a student called J a name that denigrates the whole family and questions their birth. Brother A was a couple of steps ahead of him on the stairwell and overheard the comment. He turned and hit the boy knocking him down the steps and into the arms of a football coach who was coming behind him. Coach Jones took both of them to the office and told them to stand there until the principal could be summonsed. While talking to the two students to get to the bottom of the problem, the principal was holding brother A's RIGHT arm. Brother told the principal that the student had called his brother J an SOB. Upon which the student said, "That's a lie". Suddenly, with lightening swiftness, A hit the student in the nose with his left fist resulting in a broken nose for the foul mouthed student.

I have recently learned that a school board member convinced the principal to not expel the student for fighting.

Blood is thicker than water. Brothers involved in sibling rivalry still hate a common enemy more than they hate each other.

Other than the broken nose, this story has a happy ending. The brothers have loved each other and their families have shared many events over more than sixty years. I don't remember what Mom thought about this, since she served a time as president of the PTA but I think she would have thought, though not said, "Son, I am proud of you."

Cousin Carlos

Carlos Wall was my cousin. When we were small his dad rode us in a wagon pulled by a goat. Later we went to the river for picnics in the back of an old hearse that Mr. Wall owned. Carlos and I would sell scrap iron to get a quarter to go to the movies. We grew up together and finally ended in high school and on the football team. Carlos was the center who snapped the ball to me when I was punting.

One day we had apparently found a lot of scrap iron or something because we had some real money. Like nearly three dollars. Somebody had the bright idea of going down town to Gem Drug Store and purchasing a banana split. This thing was in one of those long bowls, it had a whole banana, three flavors of ice cream, chocolate syrup, nuts, whipped cream, and cherries on top. We each bought one of these monsters. Loved every bite of it!

We walked up 8th Street to Etowah High School and dressed for football practice. Coach Stalins was a tough man. He thought stopping for a drink of water was for sissies.

We were going through all the drills and not feeling well. Soon both Carlos and I were on the side line with our heads near the grass and vomiting our heads off. Did we get to leave practice and get dressed? No! When all the banana spit, lunch, and breakfast was on the side line, we went back to the drills. Maybe that is why we were called the Piledrivers.

Football Banquet and Car Keys

It was football banquet night for the Piledrivers of Etowah High School. In this town the sidewalks are rolled up at dark. Youth complain that there is nothing to do. Someone decided on this night, after the banquet, we should all pile in cars and go to Parksville Lake in Poke County on the Hiwassee River.

I hate to admit it, but I did not have a local girl friend at the time but this "sister" who was a member of the same church as I was, agreed to go with me to the banquet. In another car on this trip was the son of our pastor. I was with Judy Whitfield.

To get down to the lake we had to walk on a narrow gravel path several yards, and it was through a patch of trees. After some time by the water's edge, still in banquet clothing, we decided to drive back to town some 8 or 10 miles. Our pastor's son discovered that he did not have his car keys. He became angry and began to use some language never heard at church. My date, a very religious girl, chastised the preacher's son for his language. Then she told him that he should be praying instead of cursing. That really made him angry and the language got worse.

Some of the experienced thieves in the crowd told him they could hotwire the car and get them back to town. So we started up the trail and it was now pitch black dark.

No we did not have flashlights. Youth don't plan they just DO.

Judy had taken off her high heel shoes. About half way up the trail my barefoot date, who believed in prayer, stepped on the car keys. She found them with her toes! She picked the keys up and jangled them in the face of the preacher's son and said, "I told you that you should pray."

Maybe it was just a coincident but coincidence is God's way of remaining anonymous.

I do not remember that Judy was even thanked for recovering the keys. Embarrassed people seldom express the emotion of thankfulness. Just believe that they really are thankful and be grateful that you were able to help.

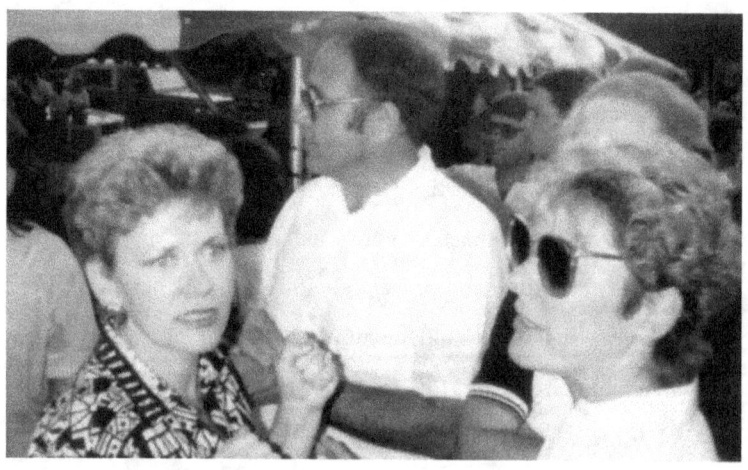

The Principal Was My Friend

Mr. Dean Holden came to Etowah High School as principal. He was young and vigorous. His football cheer was, "Go, big red". I had two incidents that endeared Mr. Holden to me.

Mr. Holden wanted to keep the school clean and it was not beneath his dignity to go down the hall way picking up paper and other trash to achieve cleanliness. On my part it was probably juvenile cuteness but I began to imitate him, especially when I thought he would see me. I would begin way at the end of the hall opposite him and begin picking up paper as I went to the central stairwell. Obviously he would see me being MR. CLEAN.

One day during a school assembly he called me to the stage and announced to the student body what a fine citizen I was and presented me with money for a hamburger steak dinner at a local restaurant. A fine example I was, even with not so good a motive.

The second incident was more serious. We had a teacher who last name was Kelley and some students made fun of her by making the sound of a machine gun. (Machine Gun Kelley) One day between classes a group of guys began making the sound as Mrs. Kelley came up the stairs. She stopped at the top, gathered up about 10 boys, including me and marched us to the office. Being the youngest of nine boys, I had learned a few things about getting spanked. BE LAST! Mrs. Kelley insisted to the principal that we needed to be punished for being disrespectful. He paddled all those guys in front of me. As they had all left the room I stepped up and told him that I could not make that sound of the machine gun and had no intention of being punished. He put his arm around my shoulder and asked me to walk out side with him. He opened the trunk of his car and handed me a pair of baseball shoes. They were my size. I never knew how he knew that I did not have baseball cleats and was on the team. I suppose that is what good principals do. They learn the needs of the students and provide what they need. I needed baseball shoes more than I needed to be paddled. For the nine or so of your guys in front of me, you got exactly what you deserved for being disrespectful. Arataratarat or something like that.

Jack Goes to College

On the other end of Scott Avenue lived the Bryan family, mother, father, Ruby and Jack. The family owned a paint store in down town Etowah. They had a clay tennis court, the only one in town. Both young people were very athletic.

As if I needed another one, Jack was like a big brother to me. He took us to away football games and things like that. He was way ahead of the Big Brother program. But then he went off to college at Georgia Tech. While there he had a call from God to enter the ministry. He left Georgia that night and went to Carson Newman College. As a very young boy I remember once he brought home with him this beautiful young lady. I think that is when I decided I wanted to go to college. (Beautiful women)

Jack later preached at New Bethel church which was about 6 miles into the country. While doing door to door visitation in that community some folk told him it was too far to walk to New Bethel from their house. So Jack started walking to New Bethel from Etowah. He would leave very early on Sunday morning. He did many unusual things in ministry. Later in life he became minister to all the prisoners in Tennessee prisons.

Finally he established Miracle Lake near Etowah and runs a Christian training program for recovering men. Jack has influenced hundreds of lives in a positive way.

Jack Bryan is my Christian hero of the faith. It was because of his life and witness that I chose to attend Carson Newman

College. Because of that choice we have been able to do mission trips to many places in the world. As I write this we are in Cape Town, South Africa celebrating our 50th wedding anniversary. Today we worked with the children in a poverty ridden area called Mountain View. Thank you Jack for a life well lived.

I also had the opportunity to watch two of Jack's children attend Carson Newman College. They were in all ways acorns from the big oak tree of a man.

The Reverend Doctor H. Cowan Ellis

Dr. Ellis was a young pastor. He had bright red hair, a great smile and a brilliant mind. It fascinated the young people that Pastor Ellis could pray on Sunday mornings for five minutes. About all we knew to pray was, "God is great, God is good, let us thank Him for our food". Maybe a little more, but not much.

What we did know was to sit in the back under the balcony. There we could hold hands, write notes, and whisper. One Sunday morning there had apparently been too much of the whispering and Dr. Ellis wanted to bring that to our attention. So, he called on a youth for the closing prayer by saying, "Jimmy Mulkey, will you lead us in the prayer of dismissal". There was a silence that seemed an eternity. I had not heard Jimmy or any other youth say a prayer in "Big Church". Finally, with a loud, strong voice, Jimmy prayed, "DISMISSED!"

That was before he became the hometown hero by running a 98 yard touchdown as the clock expired to end the game. Not bad for an interior defensive lineman. Jimmy would grow up to work in Russia for fifteen years or so, and he helped write the disarmament treaty. I'm sure he had longer prayers.

In our middle school years there was an occasion to be in the Chattanooga area for some kind of church event and we were returning to Etowah. I was in the car with Dr. Ellis and continued to encourage him to pass the cars in front of us, which he did. Then he got pulled over by a police officer. The policeman was in somewhat of an arrogant mood and said to Dr. Ellis, "Do you have a pilot's license?" Dr. Ellis replied calmly, "Yes". He opened his wallet and handed his pilot's license to the officer. Seeing that his smart aleck question was rebuffed, he told Dr. Ellis to go on, but to slow down.

Dr. Ellis would go on to be the pastor of First Baptist Church in Charlottesville, Virginia for many years. In 2012 he celebrated his 70th year in the ministry, at age 93.

High School Graduation

Being the last of nine sons, eight of which graduated from Etowah High School, it was a big deal when I graduated. I believe I heard the teachers say when I entered as a freshman, "Thankfully, here comes the last one of the Bull's". But this was my night. I was 11th in my graduating class. The top ten were seated first and then they started alphabetically. When my name was called they asked me to stop on the stage while they called my mother to the edge of the stage. They presented her with a bouquet of roses. (It was nine or twelve) Finally they called me to center stage to receive my diploma and my 12th perfect attendance award. I loved school and was blessed with good health.

Student Days at Carson Newman College

Is it better to THINK or Obey?

If you stand in front of Fite Administration building at Carson Newman facing Butler Dormitory, you will see a maple tree at the edge of the sidewalk leading up to Butler.

When that tree was planted the maintenance supervisor told an employee to water it every day. As he inspected later he found that the tree had not been watered. He called the employee to the spot, pointed to the base of the tree and said, "The next day you fail to water that tree, you will be fired." The next day when the supervisor drove in to park at Fite, he saw the worker across the street with a water hose in one hand and an umbrella in the other hand. It was pouring rain.

The worker had been 100 per cent obedient but was a literal interpretation of the command really what the supervisor wanted? Studies of developmental levels of moral development indicate that this is the lowest level. Obey but do not think.

In the summer after my freshman year of college I lived in Alexandria, Virginia with my brother, Anthony, while Barbara was doing summer mission work in Florida.

My job was at Norton and Company where we rendered bones and scrap meat that we picked up from grocery stores in the Washington D.C. area. My job was to do whatever I was told to do I was good at that even before I was married. One assignment I received from the owner was, "Paint the window frames on the north side of the building". I began on the third floor sitting in a swing hoist with a rope wrapped around a hook. I learned to take two brushes up there just in case one fell. It is a long way to pull one's self up. On the ground level the windows extended somewhat into the basement and they appeared to be new aluminum, which I painted. That side of the building had all green window frames.

When Mr. Norton came to inspect the job, a little look of shock came on his face and he said, "I didn't want the new aluminum windows painted." I think my response was, "You said all the windows on the north side". He did not reprimand me any further.

I think I should have stopped painting when I got to the ground level to ask a clarifying question like, "Do you want the aluminum windows painted?" When our moral development moves to a higher level we learn to ask questions without obeying literally.

I do not believe I would have stood in the rain to water a tree, even as a rising sophomore.

Pearl's Pigeons

Pearl McHan was the college dietician and she was totally involved in the life of the college. One year she planned a great May Day celebration. I was a student employee at the cafeteria and assisted with the program. It began a few days earlier when Miss Mc told the maintenance supervisor that she needed pigeons. He took some whiskey, soaked some corn and put the mix in the attic of Henderson building. The next day he went up in the attic and came down with a crate full of pigeons. At the cafeteria we dyed those big birds better than any that would come later on Sesame Street.

On the day of the festival I was on the ground behind the stage which had a huge rainbow across it. My job was to open the crate, on cue, to release the multicolored birds and they were to fly through the rainbow. It was beautiful but one bird was still a little tipsy and it stopped on the rainbow. The other birds flew off in seeming slow motion. It was at the end of watching the beautiful girls in their pastel evening gowns wind the ribbons around the pole. Barbara wore a green dress.

After the event we stayed to clean the area and that took about 30 minutes. Suddenly we heard a voice up near Henderson just yelling with excitement. He came running toward us with a rather expensive camera in hand. He was yelling to us about getting a picture of a rare tropical bird that must be migrating through the area. He obviously had not been at the May Day celebration and we did not have the heart to tell him any different. In those days, film was sent off to be developed. Maybe Mr. Chitwood, mathematics professor and master bird watcher, looked at the photo and helped the lad to know a dyed pigeon did not come from the tropics this May.

The Early Years with Barbara

First Year Teacher

It was 1964 and I was a first year teacher at Kingsley Elementary School in Sullivan County, Tennessee. There were two memorable events that year involving science which was my worst subject. In the spring of the year I got some tadpoles from the creek so the sixth graders could watch them change into frogs. I noticed how thin the underside of the tadpoles were and that I could see the internal organs functioning. In preparing transparencies for my mathematics class I had this sudden inspiration for a teachable moment. I would put a tadpole in a dish on the overhead projector so the class, as a whole, could watch this wonder of nature. When science class started I put the tadpole in the dish and placed in on the overhead projector. For a couple of minutes the students were entranced watching the heartbeat of the tadpole and then the unthinkable happened. The heart beat stopped cold! Or should I say the heart beat stopped HOT from the lamp of the overhead projector. The students gasped at the last heartbeat. They were probably the first sixth grade class to witness the death of a tadpole via overhead projector.

I got up the nerve to have my first field trip. We would go to King College to the observatory to see the planets. That evening the sky was overcast, with rain predicted. But being the young optimist, I gave the go ahead for the trip when the professor promised that we could at least see some slides of the planets.

On the patio of the observatory we saw a tiny hole in the clouds and the professor aligned the telescope and the students and their parents lined up for a look. Last in line, I took a look at the planet and the clouds completely covered the area and nothing was visible. We did go inside for viewing more planets via slides.

I took the children for a science field trip but did it with some faith.

Punishment to Fit the Crime

In 1964 I began teaching in rural Sullivan County, just up the road from Kingsport. Mine was a sixth grade class across the hall from the fifth grade class whose teacher was up in years, skinny and frail. She was a wonderful and kind person but in her class was a young man who was also up in years due to being detained down the grades. He was a discipline problem. One day he was particularly bad and Mrs. (name withheld) called me into the hall way and whispered to me the offense of this young man and told me that she did not have the strength to administer proper punishment. She asked if I would do the honor. Of course, anything to assist the elderly! I was a first year teacher and wanted to be a team player. She handed to me a plywood board that was at least as old as she was.

The young man took the position appropriate to the expected event like he had been here before. His hands were touching near the ankles. His rear was high in the air. On the second swat some sawdust started falling to the floor from the plywood paddle. Glancing in Mrs._____'s direction for a signal to continue or discontinue, I saw her head going wildly from side to side like a windshield wiper in a rain storm, indicating that I was to stop. Only two licks for a major offense?

That was the only time that year that she asked for the assistance of the new teacher who was anxious to be a team player.

At the end of the first year of teaching, I left to go to seminary. Sure wish I could have taught the next year to see "the young man" in my sixth grade class but maybe he learned enough just being next door to me.

In 1972 when I started teaching at Carson Newman College, I had a female student from that sixth grade class as my advisee. Her grandparents lived next door to us in Jefferson City.

Who is the Better Driver?

After graduation from college we went to North Dakota for summer missions and during that summer Ms. B's mom called the superintendent's office every day to ask if I had a job. Finally, to get her to stop calling, he said, "yes." So we moved to Sullivan County to a mobile home about six miles from the Brown farm.

That winter as we were teaching we looked forward to a snow so we could sit on our hill and watch the beauty of snow. We also knew that we could go the six miles and get some real home cooked food. The snow didn't seem so bad that day, so off we went in our Mercury Marauder. We had just made the next to the last turn on the narrow road approaching the railroad crossing which was only wide enough for one car. I saw an approaching car crossing the railroad tracks, so I edged over to let it pass. I edged over and then slid some more and was in a shallow ditch. I tried forward, reverse, forward, reverse and was hopelessly stuck.

Ms. B suggested that I walk the rest of the way to the farm and borrow Uncle Bob's farm tractor and come back with tractor and chain to pull the car out. It seemed like a good plan at the time. I put on my coat and hood and walked toward the farm. I had crossed the railroad, walked a couple of blocks and turned the last corner to go up the hill to the house. By this time I was fairly exhausted with the snow blowing in my face. Behind me I heard a car horn, so I got as near the ditch as possible and looked back. It was MY car.

Ms. B said she got tired of sitting there and decided to try to get the car out of the ditch. She said with a smile, "It drove right out". And out went my masculine superiority.

She had learned to drive on a farm tractor going less than one mile an hour and I learned in a car with a drunk sitting on the passenger side passed out. Learning on a farm tractor or lawn mower is the better way for young people to learn to drive.

The Orange Peel

Working in the college cafeteria for Pearl McHan left little to no room for foolishness. It was, after all, a business and she was all business. However, behind her back there was sometimes some playfulness. (The worker who changed the menu board from "Deviled Crabs" to "Deviled Arabs" was fired) One of the games that we played was to take a small piece of orange peel and squeeze it near the eye of a co-worker. The recipient would cry a little bit and that was it. No harm no foul.

One day at the farm in Bristol, I remembered this dumb trick from my college days. It must have been Christmas vacation because we had oranges. I squeezed a peel in Barbara's eye and she began to cry a little. Her mother thought she cried a lot. She said the only harsh words she ever said in my presence. "She can only see in one eye and it needs to be protected".

This was way different from the day Mrs. Brown took me blackberry picking when Barbara and I were dating. That conversation is a family secret. Believe me, she was a wonderful mother-in-law and she did not want her girl to be crying. I guess I should be glad that she has not been present all the time over the last 40 to 50 years. She may have killed me. There have been many more smiles than tears.

Tools of the Trade

Granddaddy Brown. Let me explain the name. Having had my daddy die before I was born, I never called anyone daddy. Barbara's dad was named Shirley Sutton Brown. I could not deal with calling a man Shirley. His close male friends called him SS. That was way too disrespectful for me to call a man his age SS. Barbara wanted me to just call him Dad. I could not bring myself to do that. So, when I wanted to talk with him, I looked directly in his eyes so he knew I was talking to him. That went or for 4 or 5 years until Brad was born. What is Brad going to call his grandfather? They settled on Granddad, if Brad was to learn to call him granddad that was what I would model for him.

Granddad had a saw mill on the back of the farm which he operated with the next door neighbor, Mr. Orfield, who we all called "Uncle Bob".

One day, not long after I had joined the family, I walked to the back of the 20 acres to OBSERVE the saw mill in the hollow. The key word here is "observe" with no intention of working. The saw blade was roaring and the two men were running the log through and catching planks on the other end. It looked like pure fun and they did it as a hobby.

Granddad yelled to me and pointed up on the hillside toward a log and said, "Roll that next log down here".

I walked up the hill and stood there looking at an oak log that was 20-30 feet long and about18-20 inches in diameter. I got

down on my knees behind the log to give it push. It may have moved a quarter of an inch. After a few of my struggles, Granddad saw that I was not going to roll it down. I saw him walking up the hill. He picked up a pole that had a metal hook on the end. It was a tool I had never seen before. It is called a log roller. He slapped the hook into the back side of the log, put ONE hand on the pole, looked at me and flipped his wrist and the log rolled down the hill to the saw mill.

    In all work you need to have the right tool and know how to use it. One philosopher, Maslow I think, said, "If the only tool you have is a hammer, you tend to treat everything as if it were a nail". When I was in teacher education, my goal was to be sure the future teachers had the tools and knew how to use them.

Barbara and the Bra Ad

We were college freshmen when we met in 1960. This was a time when national publications were reflecting the sexual revolution of the day. Advertisements in magazines were becoming more realistic in picturing what in the days before Madonna were called UNDER wear. One such ad was for the Maiden Form bra in a national magazine like LOOK or LIFE. A movie star was riding on the back of a fire truck, hanging on with one hand, looking back with the caption: I dreamed I went to the fire in my Maiden Form bra. (Jane Russell possibly) The next ad had a picture of the movie star holding the horn of a bull and the caption was: I dreamed I took the bull by the horn in my Maiden Form bra. Due to the photo and name of the bull, I thought it was the  perfect gift for my girlfriend so I tore one from a magazine and took it to Barbara's dorm and gave it to her. She taped it inside her closet door in the dorm. When the dorm matron made an inspection she saw the photo in the closet. Barbara was given demerits for having a "lewd" photo in her room. Never mind that it was on every news stand in America. It was still lewd at CNC.

Many years later, in fact after Bethany was married, we rented her in-laws condo in Daytona for a week. While there we went out one evening in search of some ice cream. We located an ice cream store and there in the front window was a life size cow with horns. PHOTO TIME! I had Barbara hold the horn of the cow and took the photo. She had on a pink sweater and the picture was pure joy. It is now the screen saver on this computer. I emailed the photo to Brad. He went on line and located the original ad and photo copied it. That picture is behind the door in our bedroom to this day.

I guess the demerit Barbara received in college was worth it for all the fun we have with this story.

Girls were not allowed on campus in shorts so when we played tennis Barbara had to wear a rain coat to the tennis court.

The dorm matron saw us leaving one day and asked, "Do you think it is going to rain?"

How the times have changed. Now the girls sun bathe across the street from the dorm on the lawn of First Baptist Church and there is no one to question it. Our society fought the sexual revolution and lost.

The Jar of Rhubarb

Ms B and I were the first college students in the U S to be allowed, by the Home Mission Board of the Southern Baptist Convention, to drive a car to a summer mission assignment. We were married and rising seniors. Mature I'm sure for our age. Ha!

We were also able to deliver other students to their destinations, including Colorado Springs and on to North Dakota. In Colorado the students were kept in a building during orientation but since we were married we were given a large tent in which to sleep. The first night it came a hail storm and we nearly froze to death. The only heat being our bodies and a heating pad which we hung from the light bulb. It almost reached the bed.

Ms B had brought along a Ball fruit jar filled with home canned strawberry rhubarb preserves. While in Hallock, Minnesota we stayed in the home of two families. In preparation for departure Ms B gifted our host family with that jar of preserves. (We liked the one family enough to name our son after their son, Brad.)

The next summer we were honored to return to the same churches but we stayed with different host families. At the end of our six weeks we packed for departure and the host family gifted us with A JAR OF RHUBARB. Yes, it was the same Ball fruit jar that we had given a host family last year. We figured that every event that happened in that church a different family had received that rhubarb. It circulated back to us. What goes around, comes around.

Ms B was pregnant with Brad when we received the jar of rhubarb. Maybe that explains why he hated the green slime just as much as I do. I suppose the lesson I learned was, "Give a gift that you would like to receive".

Flat Tire in the Bayou

We had a loaded Mercury headed for Forth Worth, Texas and were passing through Louisiana. On a long stretch of nothing but swamp we had a flat tire on the back left. In that model car the spare tire was in the bottom of the trunk. I took all the material from the trunk to the grassy knoll beside the road while watching carefully for snakes and alligators. After digging out the spare tire and jack, I removed the flat tire, put on the spare and let the car jack down. I listened to a whistling sound as the spare went flat. At that time I did not know John Dewey's pragmatic five steps to problem solving. I knew I had a pregnant wife, two flat tires, very little money and a great fear of snakes.

I evaluated the situation and knew I needed help, when along came a native of the area. I asked him where there was a service station and he pointed west and said, "There is one beyond the river." I questioned if he could take me there with two flat tires. His reply startled me. "I ain't never been beyond the river". He had never been outside the parish in which he was born.

My mother and grandparents sang the song, "When They Ring Those Golden Bells" in which they sang about a land beyond the river. But they were singing about the symbolism of crossing the Jordan into the Promised Land and that represented crossing the river of death and going into heaven. Now this man in Louisiana sounded just like my ancestors except that he meant the only way he was leaving this parish was straight up and if I wanted a tire fixed beyond the river; that was my problem.

Eventually a more traveled native came along who drove a school bus but was currently in his pickup truck. He drove us to a little town to a business, both of which will remain unnamed. That business said they were not a regional store and could not honor our warranty. We had to purchase a tire at full price and hope we had no more trouble until we got to Dallas and a "regional" store. About 50 years later, I still do not enjoy trading with that store. They are beyond the river.

Bradley Wayne Winds Up

We moved to Fort Worth, Texas and Brad was born in Harris Hospital on December 2, 1965. Hospital regulations in those days were very strict and dads were forbidden to hold the new born baby until the nurse brought mother and baby to the curb at dismissal from the hospital. One man who was a seminary student was found hiding in a closet trying to slip in to hold his new born. He was removed from the hospital. I on the other hand, being a rule follower, went to the big window to see Brad through the window. All the new born babies were asleep except Brad. As I watched and glowed, someone said, "Look at that one holding his head up". I smiled but said nothing about the "turtle" being mine. Later he would show his hatred for nap time in kindergarten.

We didn't have a lot of cash while I was a student at Southwestern Baptist Theological Seminary but somehow we got enough change ahead to purchase a windup music box. It was made by Fisher Price. Years later it would be worn enough for us to see the wood behind the covering.

We worked at Lena Pope Children's home and Brad had a room. We would wind the music box and put it beside him in the bed as he went to sleep. One night the music box played on and on and on. I told Ms B, "That thing cannot possibly be playing this long".

I got up from bed and looked through the door in time to see him winding his toy music box. Before age one he would rather wind than sleep.

Brad's First/Only Drunk

Soon after Bradley was born we moved to a job at Lena Pope Children's Home on West Rosedale Street in Fort Worth Texas. We had the responsibility of several teen age boys. Later we were promoted to caretakers of the Wellness Center and Brad had his own room. We took care of sick children, especially at night when the nurse was not there.

On Sunday we rode with all the children on the bus to Broadway Baptist Church. This church had wonderful facilities and the nursery was so clean you could eat off the floor. Also, it was special because they had a medical doctor who worked in the nursery.

One Sunday morning we were called out of our Sunday School class and told the doctor wanted to see us in the nursery. We anxiously rushed to the nursery to begin being interrogated by the doctor. Had Brad been sick? He seems a little strange. Strange in deed with his eyes rolled back. Barbara said, "Yes, he had taken a little cold and this morning I gave him some cough medicine." "No," I interrupted, "This morning I gave the cough syrup to Brad." The doctor just smiled and said, "He's drunk".

As far as we know, that was the only time for Brad to be intoxicated. The remainder of his highs at church have been Spiritual.

Saturday Night at Lena Pope Children's Home

Lena Pope Children's Home had a large building called Baby Land where the infants were kept. Some children lived in the home from near birth until completing high school. It became obvious to us that some of these children had never experienced things that most children take for granted. In fact, some of them had never seen an egg cracked before being cooked. One special event that we thought every child should experience was making home made ice cream. I remembered as a boy in New Zion community that my brother Marcel rode our horse to Etowah and returned with a 100 pound block of ice from the icehouse. I watched my older brothers crank the ice cream freezer. What a treat on a hot day, way before air conditioning, to have ice cream. We wanted the boys in the children's home to have that experience.

We got a hand crank freezer, the ingredients, ice and salt and prepared to make ice cream in the yard beside the boys' wing of the home. The deal was this: If you do not help crank, you do not help eat. All the boys were anxious to help crank. As a child, I remember volunteering to crank first. Why wait until the crank is so hard to turn? Well, on this day, all the boys turned the crank, some 12 of them. However, it was not working like it was supposed to. Even after the last boy had taken a turn the handle could be turned easily. Finally I suggested to Ms. B that we open it and just let the boys drink it.

We opened the lid to find that the ice cream was so hard the paddle could not be removed. It was frozen solid and it had been turning inside the cylinder. It was the hardest ice cream I have ever seen, before or since. It must have been the reaction of the salt to the hot Texas sun. As we tried to cut the ice cream out from around the paddle the boys began to enjoy their first homemade ice cream.

Sunday Night at Lena Pope Children's Home

During the time we worked with the teenage boys we had many wonderful experiences. Our training in education and personal experience with family was tested to the limit with these boys.

One Sunday afternoon a group of the boys came to me for a serious discussion. They believed that they had arrived at the age where they could make decisions on their own. They now were too old to attend Sunday night worship services. I told them that tonight we would stay home from church

Late that evening the bus pulled out of the drive way of the Children's Home headed for Broadway Baptist Church down town Fort Worth. Only some teenage boys and I stayed at home. I instructed the boys to remove all the chairs and tables from the dining hall and into the dormitory hall ways. That done, I sprayed water on the floor with a garden hose, soaped it down and the boys began to scrub the dirty wax from the floor. Then they mopped the floor dry. They waxed the floor and waited for it to dry. (The bus had long since returned from church) After the wax had dried, the boys retuned all the tables and chairs to the dining hall. This room would seat about ninety people.

We went to bed after 10 o'clock.

The next Sunday afternoon was a beautiful warm day and as the time approached for the bus to arrive to take us to church the teenage boys were sitting on the sidewalk benches waiting.

They seemed to have developed a real desire for Sunday night worship.

Ignorance

Phillip Gulley in his *Front Porch Tales* wrote, "I never attribute to malice anything that can adequately be explained as stupid." At the insistence of my wife, I am including this story that she has told many more times than I have.

At Lena Pope Children's home we had been promoted from Teenage Boys wing to the wellness center. The house just up the street housed the Teenage Girl's building and their house parents were J D and Jackie Scolaro, our friends from college days.

One night JD phoned us and was in a complete panic. There was a rat in their apartment. I loaded my 22 pistol and ran over to J D's. The door had a towel under it to prevent the escape of the monster mouse. They slipped me into the room and it looked like a tornado had passed through. They KNEW the rat was still in this room. On top of the book case, which now had little of anything on it, sat a piece of drift wood painted black that came from Cherokee Lake. Suddenly that rat jumped up on that drift wood and just sat there. J D was turning red. I took aim and fired a round of 22. The sound apparently rattled the rat and he sat. I shot again and he jumped and I fired while it was in mid air. After 6 shots the rat was still on the run. We would have to kill it with a broom.

Unbeknown to me, the building was offset and the wall I was shooting into was the wall of the girls' room. Little did I know that mirrors were falling on the floor of that room and the girls were getting under their beds.

The next morning I was sitting on the door steps of the executive director's office when he arrived for work. I related the message to him of how terrified J D was of rats and that I was trying to help him. Not one of the girls was dead!

Mr. Leland Hacker, who had promoted me from custodian to Education Director, kind of smiled an understanding nod of youth stupidity. It was never mentioned again; that is except when Barbara wants me to come down a notch or two.

The Olive Colored Kindergartner

It was in the late 1960's in a Southern city and in a private church related elementary school. It was all white and we were on the faculty. I was teaching 6-8th grades in a building that was two city blocks from the old slave market. During the May race riots thirteen people were killed and part of the city was burned. I looked from my class room window at the smoke rising. National Guard units patrolled the streets as we drove to and from school. Our church had traditionally stationed a guard at the door to prevent people of color from attending. Our school had K-8 grades, all white.

One day a beautiful blond lady came to the school office to enter her son in kindergarten. He was an attractive olive colored boy with a big smile. The mother had a slight British accent. The son was enrolled and began attending.

After a time the father came to school one day to pick up the son. To the shock of the school secretary, the father was very black. He was a former military man who had married in England while in service. The shock reverberated to the principal's office and eventually to the school's board of trustees. In their wisdom of the day, they decided the best thing to do was to ask the family to remove the boy from our white school. The first assigned deacon refused to go do this assignment. The second man, a close friend of ours, started to the house and had a flat tire on his car.

While fixing the tire, on his knees beside the car he was inspired to discontinue his quest.

At the end of the year the kindergarten had a graduation ceremony which was held in the gymnasium. As the program began, in came the olive complexioned boy carrying the flag of the United States of America.

This was the quietest racial integration that took place in the South.

Crazy at Curtis

At Curtis Baptist Church in Augusta, Georgia I was teaching middle school and also director of the youth program. We were blessed to have a large gymnasium and basketball courts in the parking lot. Also we had very supportive parents who came to many events. One evening as we watched the children and youth playing, a new youth came who was not a member. He entered the building by jumping down on his hands, turning a flip to his feet down the entire gym floor and returning with reverse flips. He was a physical specimen. He was short and stocky! I was later to learn that he was recently released from Reedville State Hospital for the Mentally Insane. For the life of me, I do not know why they let him out. He had seen one or both of his parents killed when he was a child. He had deep psychological problems.

One Sunday morning this young man appeared at church, way under dressed with shorts and tennis shoes but that was not the bad part. He had prepared placards with his message to the world and he wanted to get on the podium and deliver his message while our service was on television. My pastor had other ideas. He wanted me to keep the young man in the office and away from our television ministry.

I invited the young man to come with me and he came carrying his placards. We sat in the office. He was in an easy chair and I was in the office chair behind the desk. We talked of several things and he stood up, pulled a switch blade knife from his pocket, flipped the long blade out and walked around the desk to me. He used the blade to push my tie to one side, put the blade against the button on my shirt and said, "I could kill you before you could move". I was not moving! On the outside, I was not moving. In my heart I was moving and I believe I was praying. Eventually he closed the knife and returned to his seat. We began hearing the singing of the invitation hymn and the young man said to me, "You have done your job, keeping me here". He got up and left. I sat there for a little while being grateful to be alive. Looking back, I was not paid enough for what I did at Curtis Baptist Church; at least not that day.

The New Fangled Thing at School

When my daddy died the family lived on a dairy farm in Bradley County. At a 4th of July celebration in Etowah, I mentioned to my brother Marcel that I had no memory of the dairy farm because I was just a baby when we moved to New Zion community in McMinn County. Marcel suggested we drive down there so I could see the place so we jumped in his car for the 30 minute drive. We arrived at the dairy farm and were greeted by the current owners. The old milk barn was about gone and the owner agreed to give me a large stone from the foundation's corner. I had the stone engrave with my name and birth date. The stone now sits in New Zion community at the place we call The Spring.

On this trip to Bradley County, Marcel related to me the following story which I had never heard about my older brothers. In the 1930's the school principal had called a parents' meeting to explain something new at the school where four of the older brothers attended. At the meeting the principal illustrated the use of a hand cranked pencil sharpener. Dad got the boys together back at the dairy farm house and warned them to NOT use the newfangled thing at school. He told them that he would continue to sharpen their pencils to the correct nib with his pocket knife.

With pencils costing two cents each, times four boys that would be eight cents a week if they were to grind down a pencil a week. At the wage he earned, that money for pencils would be a large portion of his income. What would dad think today if he went to see the students grinding down pencils with electric pencil sharpeners? Added to that, the pencils of today are not two cents

but more like 25 to 50 cents. Wasted wood!

Ironically this event took place just as the Progressive Education movement was being started by John Dewey. My dad's prognostication about pencil sharpeners could be multiplied a thousand times over for the damage done by the Progressive Education Movement.

Brad's Play-Doh Elephant

We moved to Augusta, Georgia when Brad was five years old and we rented a house from the Wilson's family. We were in the country and had to create our own entertainment. We played pitch and things like that outside. Inside we read lots of books and played word games. One evening we were playing in the floor and Play-Doh got into the fun. I was pretty good at making figures and as we messed around I made a fairly decent representation of an elephant. It had a great long truck, big ears and short curly tail. I had a small amount of Play-Doh left over so I quickly made some round balls of elephant excrement and dropped it behind the elephant. Brad lay on the floor laughing so long and hard that he wet his pants.

Brad's First Eye Examination

When Brad was a baby we worked in Lena Pope Children's Home in Fort Worth. I remember holding him in my arms on the front lawn one day and he was just learning to talk. He said, "Plane" and was looking in the sky. I looked and listened and saw nothing and heard nothing. In a little while I saw a spot in the sky and barely heard a helicopter.

I knew then that he had great vision.

Somewhat later, when he was about six years old, I took him for his first eye examination. It may have been when he was starting first grade. We spend the necessary time in the outer office and were ushered into the examination room for the other wait time. Brad was of course, curious about everything in the room and I gave him pretty free rein as long as he did not touch the instruments.

Finally the assistant came in to do the preliminary things before the doctor's arrival.

She prepared the instruments, put Brad in the chair and turned on the light for the wall chart. Her first question was, "Can you read the bottom line?" His response was, "Patent pending, Philadelphia comma P E N N period." She looked in shock like she had never before had a patient "read the bottom line".

Have you noticed that many times in life there is a problem because we ask the wrong question and assume the hearer understands? And sometimes, when people do understand they can still give cute answers.

Party of Ten

Several members of our extended family went to a popular restaurant in Knoxville where the head waitress would ask, "How many in your party?" "What is the name?" My niece who was high school age was not thrilled with the family name BULL, so she asked to me not tell the waitress that the party was BULL which would be called out over the loud speaker in the restaurant. I did not say bull in making the reservations. Shortly, over the loud speaker it was announced, "Party of Smith and Wesson, your table is ready".

Apparently the waitress was not familiar with firearms. I shot our way through without embarrassing a vulnerable high school female bull.

The Years on the Carson Newman Faculty

Prayer and Desperate Prayer at Graduation

Being a first year faculty member is like being a freshman in high school. I was the low man on the totem pole. At academic convocations the faculty with the most years of service marched in first and sat in front. The pecking order continued to the back where we green horns sat. I was about dead last in 1972.

Our Academic Dean, a native of Alabama, (now deceased or this story would not be in here) thought it would be politically correct to have the first female in the history of the college to deliver the commence address. And of course she had to come from Alabama, the University of Alabama. Her advanced degree was in Higher Education. She was determined to show her advanced degree in a 45 minute address. The May weather was hot and overcast when she started her lecture. Then the lightning began to strike in the distance. As the storm drew closer her conclusion did not. Fearing that lightning was going to hit the goal post at the end of the football field I had, what I thought was a great idea at the time. I scribbled on a note, "Pray for rain", and handed it to a Religion professor seated in front of me. A simple request for prayer was passed down the row. I watched shoulders shake and mouths covered with snickering. As this event moved closer to the front, closer to the Academic Dean my breathing became slower and slower as I prayed that someone up there (at the front of the processional) had the good sense to put it in his/her pocket. Finally the note came to rest with a very senior faculty members on the front row. He could have almost leaned forward and handed it to the stage. I was ready to wet my pants and really pray for rain because the dean would have fired me if he could have traced the handwriting. And I knew he would try.

Several years later, Brad called one day and in an excited voice asked if I had read the current Reader's Digest. I responded that I had not. He then cited a page number. I looked it up and there was my story. The author of the Reader's Digest version of the story was Dr. Louis Ball. I called him and told him that I had originated the note. He replied that he had the $200 and none of it was mine. But he has been a lifelong friend and I owe him my job of 35 years because he helped answer my prayer for rain.

The Fire Truck

It was 1972 when we moved into an apartment complex in Jefferson City. There were five apartments upstairs and five downstairs. One day we heard some commotion and yelling that someone smelled smoke. The smoke was in an apartment downstairs. As the police arrived, the apartment manager unlocked the sliding glass door entrance. The police officer went inside about two steps and came back out declaring that he could not stand the smoke. I got on my hands and knees and crawled to the source of the smoke.

The lady of the house had been in the hospital and her husband had been throwing his dirty clothing on the bathroom floor which was also wet. When the night temperature had gotten chilly the thermostat had kicked the heat on. The heat was enough to create smoke from the wet clothing. I turned the heater off and crawled back out of the apartment.

Standing in the parking lot stood about 20 volunteer firemen from the ALL Volunteer fire department. I overheard one volunteer say to his fellow fireman, "Didn't you bring the truck?" And he responded, "NO, didn't you bring the truck?"

Unfortunately, no one remembered to bring the fire truck. Fortunately, there was not a fire. That was life in Jefferson City before the city fathers had the good sense to hire a fire chief.

Pregnant in the Berry Patch

Barbara and her good friend Martha Toomey were both about 7-8 months pregnant. We lived in the same apartment complex. Ms. Toomey was from West Virginia and the hillbilly in her sometimes got a hankering for picking blackberries. Same for Ms. B. They seemed to always have buckets ready when berries were in season. They were driving past a farm and saw briers, lots of briers and black berries. Stopping they held the barbed wire fence apart while each of them wiggled through. No small feat in their condition.

Shortly along came the owners of the property. They got out of the car and yelled at Martha to ask what she was doing. Unbeknown to her Ms B was picking near the ground behind some bushes. (I believe she was hiding but she swears not) Anyway, she was squatted down and invisible to the property owners. Martha's response to the owners, while gesturing with her arm toward her back, was, "My friend and I are just picking some berries." The owners must have been thinking that Martha was some kind of mental patient. Or maybe she still had a child's mind with an imaginary friend. Seeing her "condition" they told her to pick some more and then kindly get off their property.

This story is always brought to mind when blackberries are in bloom. Remember, when you go uninvited on to someone's property, take a friend who will stand beside you; unless there is some other reason to SQUAT.

Blackberry Pickers' Children

The blackberry patch pregnant women had a son and a daughter. We all went on a picnic out to Cherokee Dam. The son had not yet stopped sucking his thumb. As I carried him in my arms, I noticed a jar of dill pickles on the table. While everyone was busy and not looking, I slipped his entire fist down into the pickle juice and quickly walked back into the grassy area.

Shortly he popped that thumb into his mouth and suddenly began to scream and cry. His mother rushed over to see why her son was in distress. I handed him to his mother with a look of "what is going on with this child?" I feigned innocence. There was no observable evidence of anything to cause pain, EXCEPT the smell of pickle juice. I do not believe that the women ever forgave me for that joke but I do believe his thumb sucking was cut short by a month or two. I believe in psychology it is called adverse stimuli or something like that. Behavior modification!

Benita Appears Nude on Campus

Benita was born when I had been teaching at Carson Newman College for four years. Barbara McDougal was a faculty member who taught Home Economics in which she taught a course in Child Development. The Home Economics department laboratory had a table with a tilt mirror that was about two feet by six feet long. The instructor could work on the table and the class could watch in the mirror.

With a warm pan of water ready, Mrs. McDougal illustrated how to undress a baby without breaking its arms and legs. I mean undress down to the skin. She then washed the baby, Benita, dried her and then dressed her in dry clothing.

Hopefully, this lesson saved some other child from having broken limbs.

C V and Madison

The names have not been changed to protect the innocent because that would ruin the authenticity of this set of brothers who graced the Jefferson City community in the 60's and 70's of their adult years. Rumor around town was that their parents were cousins and the gene pool was defective. Today we would call them "Special". Back then we called them "Characters". College students and faculty members actually experienced these characters. Some of the students had a few laughs at the expense of those brothers.

C V had a gold watch but he could not tell time. Students would meet C V and ask him for the time. He would extend his arm in your face and say, "There it is".

Some clever students would take a nickel and a dime and show the two coins to Madison and ask, "Which is larger? If you can guess, I'll give it to you". If he said the nickel was larger, the student would laugh and hand him the nickel. One day a compassionate student tried to explain to Madison the value of money. A dime is larger than a nickel because the dime is 10 cents and the nickel is 5 cents. Madison listened as though trying to understand the concept and then his wisdom dawned and he explained to the student, "If I believed that I would not get any nickels."

Now you tell me, who was smarter?

In our days on the faculty Ms. B washed Madison's clothes on a weekly basis and we often went to the nursing home to bring him to church. He was a sweet old man and he could not help it when he announced in a LOUD stage whisper during church services, "I've got to go PEE."

Wind Up Clock

When Brad was preschool age we purchased a large toy clock that would say the time out loud when you set the hands and pushed a button. It only voiced on the hour and half hour. So we set the hands, push the button and hear the clock say such as, "It's three thirty."

After we had survived a year in an apartment in Jefferson City we got the opportunity to move into Glenmore Mansion as caretakers. We were to live in 10 of the 26 rooms. The back part of the mansion was called Doll Town and it had three stories. The whole place was a little creepy to most people because it had the characteristics of a haunted house.

We recruited some friends to assist with moving day as we loaded the truck to move about five blocks. Brad's room was going to be on the top floor up three flights of creaky stairs. One friend picked up an arm load of Brad's things to carry up to the third floor. He was going there alone! As he ascended the last flight we heard a scream just after he heard someone up there say, "It's twelve o'clock". He threw the load of toys in the air and ran back down the stairs.

Now we knew that the battery had been taken out of the clock and put in the box when we were packing. A mystery faced us. We opened the box and clock to discover that the battery had rolled into the clock, in the correct positive-negative direction to activate the recorder.

That was the beginning of many mysterious events at the Glenmore Mansion where we lived for seven years and only two of Brad's friends ever managed to come there on Halloween and those two were right beside their mothers.

Brick Shot-put

For a few years we were caretakers of the 26 room Victorian mansion called Glenmore in Jefferson City. This was when Brad was a small boy. The mansion was surrounded by a tree line separating the lawn from the pasture. One day Brad and I were in the yard and saw a rabbit at the edge of the shrubs and trees about 15 to 20 yards away. The idea ran through my mind that I could throw a brick beyond the rabbit into the tree line and scare the rabbit into running toward us so Brad could see it up close and running. I launched a high throw and the rabbit moved just far enough for the brick to hit it right in the back of its head. Brad yelled, "Great shot dad!" That was before the animal rights activists came into prominence or I would have been hauled before the courts and fined for being "a great shot."

As my son-in-law wears on a tee shirt, "All God's creatures have a place, right beside my mashed potatoes.

Bats in the Belfry

One of the hazards of living in Glenmore Mansion was sharing the house with many winged mammals who usually stayed in the attic until night. One night I was taking a bath and I heard Barbara scream. I jumped out of the tub and took the four or five steps to our bedroom door with a towel in my hand. Barbara pushed me into the bedroom as she screamed, "There's a bat in there!" The door slammed behind me.

There I stood, stark naked with a towel in my hand. The bat circled the room like an airplane over Atlanta. I leaned back and forth as it circled right in front of me. Remembering the locker room days at Etowah High School, I watched, timed and popped that sucker right out of the air. It was then that I started keeping a BB gun beside the bed.

One night, Barbara's mother was visiting and slept in a room adjacent to ours. That night she got up to go to the bathroom. As she returned, she was sliding her house shoes along the wood floor. It was a ghostly sound. I was awakened just enough to keep from shooting her.

Bats do much good with eating bugs but they really need a home away from people like me.

Timmy and Granddaddy Brown's Bull

Over the years we have kept 17 foster children. Once we had three siblings, two boys and a girl. The two boys were what most people call "all boy" and sometimes a little slow to catch on. They often had more youthful energy than good judgment.

We took our family of seven to visit the Brown's farm near Bristol, Tennessee. (side note: Barbara worked in a produce store during high school and one of her customers was the father of Tennessee Ernie Ford) Mr. Brown had a 20 acre farm and several cattle. He built a yoke and two of the large animals could pull a sled.

Grandfather Brown wanted to teach Timmy a lesson, by way of a challenge to his youthful energy and his desire for money. He gave Timmy a rope and told him that if he could lasso the horns of the big cow he would receive 10 dollars. Timmy was

about 4 feet tall but he was fast. He would run toward the animal, throw the lasso and the cow would walk a few feet and continue eating grass. This process went on from midmorning until Timmy was called to lunch. He resumed his quest immediately after lunch and it continued until late afternoon. Timmy was near exhaustion. The cow was barely exercised.

Late in the afternoon Grandfather walked down to the corn crib near the barn and retrieved a pan of corn. He got the rope back from Timmy and made a sound that says, "Cow come over here". He shook the pan. Here came the cow and stuck its head into the pan to eat the corn. Grandfather laid the rode around the horn, pulled the pan aside, and started leading the big cow wherever he wanted it to go.

If only I had taken a camera to capture the look of surprise and wonder on Timmy's face that you do not catch a cow by chasing it but by feeding it. Chasing may work with a girl on the playground but not with a cow in a large pasture.

Timmy and the Snowman

We lived in Glenmore Mansion as caretakers. Beside the house there were large cow pastures. One winter it came a big soft snow and we rolled large balls of snow down a big hill and made a rather large snowman (snow person for the PC group) It took several of us to put the top piece on. It was big! That night was frigged.

The next day the children got bundled up to go out and play in the snow. I was sitting at the kitchen window observing from some 30-40 yards away from the edge of the pasture. I saw Timmy go to the top of a hill with a snow sled. Suddenly the boy in me saw what his intentions were. He wants to fly down the hill and burst our snowman. He did not realize what the temperature of the night had done to our snowman.

Off the hill he went at "break neck" speed. When the sled hit the snowman Timmy's head hit a solid block of ice. Grabbing a coat, I hurried to get to the scene of the accident.

I had to go about 70 yards included going over the fence. When I got there, out of breath, Timmy was lying on his back with his eyes closed. "Out cold" took on new meaning.

We revived him and helped him back to the house. Would he ever do such a thing again if given the chance? YES! This is what boys do. Moral judgment comes late for males.

Pancake Syrup

When you are poor you learn to make do with what you have. One of the ways we did that was to make 'homemade' pancake syrup. We would take a cup of brown sugar, put in boiling water and boil it down to a thickness that resembled Hungry Jack, at least if you have a pretty good imagination.

We had three foster children, our own two, at the time, so there were 7 of us when we went places. We went very few places in fact but one place was the Brown farm in Bristol. It was at Thanksgiving I believe and Mrs. Brown and the girls were planning and preparing meals. Ms. B I'm pretty sure suggested making pancake syrup for the next morning. The next morning they made pancakes for the now ten people who would be at the table. As I tasted my pancakes I thought it was the flattest taste I had ever had in my mouth. But I did not want to bring undue attention to my displeasure for fear of turning the children against mom's pancakes. I suffered in silence as I would later find out, so did several other adults.

That evening we were around the table again and some people asked for the beverage to be iced tea. The first swallow was enough to let one know that this was the sweetest tea ever brewed. In fact, it was pancake syrup made from brown sugar. Yes, that means that for breakfast we had put hot tea on our pancakes. They were, hot, soft, and tasteless.

Too many cooks in the kitchen can ruin the broth. The experience gave new appreciation for Hungry Jack that can be heated in the microwave, now that we have a little money.

Father's Day

Due to my gross lack of mechanical skills it was a blessing that I became a teacher because we would have been really poor if I had been forced to work with tools. That helps to explain my mild displeasure with a gift I received from one of my children one Christmas. After everyone had left I decided to use part of the Christmas vacation to put together this thing that the box indicated was a device to hold a garden hose. Maybe my garden hose had been piled up outside and they thought I needed to crank it up.

Any way I received this box. Alone in the living room, with the Christmas tree put away, I emptied the contents of the box on the floor. There were 10 plastic pieces, 100 screws and 99 nuts and assembly instructions in Spanish. Several days later, after school had resumed, I completed the assembly but for the life of me I do not know why there were still parts laying on the floor. I just put them back in the box and put the machine in the basement to wait for spring to roll up the garden hose.

Later, in as gentle way as I knew how, I said to my grown children, "Please, do not give me a gift that has to be assembled".

Being the sweet, loving offspring that they are, and understanding my lack of assembly skills, they agreed to follow my instructions.

Father's Day rolled around and I went into the front yard to confront a ton of mulch that had been delivered to my house and dumped in the yard. No assembly required.

From Out of Town

My professor from Texas Christian University, in Fort Worth, along with his wife, was moving to East Tennessee State University to his new job. Immediately after settling into their new house the wife left for a convention in Chicago. While waiting in the airport she realize that she had never looked through a "girly" magazine and she saw some of those dirty things on the rack in the book store. Being a few hundred miles away from a home that was new and where she knew no one, she submitted to the temptation to look through one of those magazines. She took a seat and looked, in shock I'm sure, at those filthy pictures.

Returning to Tennessee she was just in time to accompany her professor husband to a reception for new faculty members. Meet and greet, simple. Socializing with Kool-aid and cookie in hand she met a female faculty member who said, "Do I know you?" "No you could not possibly know me, we just moved here from Texas". The lady gave her a strange look and said, "But I know I have seen you somewhere. Let's see, ...yes, I saw you in the airport in Chicago this week." I bet her face turned the color of the Kool-aid, red or green!

The Chinese have a saying: "The night has a million eyes." Be sure one of those eyes will see you, even if you are from "Out of Town".

Trees

Barbara's dad was a lumber man in his early years. He took the new Mrs. Brown to the lumber camp where she was the cook. That was on their honeymoon. Well, people do have to work for a living some times. Anyway, I was fortunate to learn a few things from him about the lumber business and he bought a chain saw for me.

Being a college professor we were not poor but definitely not wealthy. So we cut wood for the wood stove in our basement. Heating the house with a wood fire would save some money. We had a small storage shed behind the house for the cord wood. We got wood where ever we could. One day a lady offered some free trees to me. She lived out on highway 92 beyond the high school. The deal was, one tree was rather near her house and a little dangerous. The other tree was out in the field. Brad and I started cutting. The tree in the woods seems to have been an Elm. Hard as a brick! The sun was going down and I was hurrying to finish before dark. I was so tired I was almost shaking as I hit the wedge with the sledge hammer trying to get it done. My statement to Brad was, "Why is the last one the hardest?" To which he replied, "If you leave it until morning, it will be the first one." Now there is a teenager ready to go home.

That was way before I learned another quotation, "Jesus never hurried and he was never late."

Years ago, Sam B "Frosty" Holt was in the woods with his boys and they pulled up a cherry tree, took it home and planted it in their backyard. It was right near the drive way to Mrs. Mary Elizabeth Smith's house. Some years after the passing of Frosty, Mrs. Holt asked me to take down the cherry tree because black ants were in it. . I did take it down and Rugel's furniture company made a lectern that is in Holt Fieldhouse at CNC. Later, she asked me to take down a big hemlock that was right beside her house. There was plenty of room to fall it into a wide street, which I proceeded to do. Unfortunately a mild wind began blowing and the tree was leaning toward the house. Around the corner came a car driven by my pastor; the sometimes unReverand CH Christopher. I waved him down and said, "Pastor, pray for me, that tree is leaning toward the house". His hasty reply was, "Pray, hell, did you not tie it off".

I suppose there is a time to ask for prayer and a time to refrain from asking for prayer, especially if you're doing something stupid. That is when most people say, "Bless his heart".

Geographically Challenged

Teaching college in the 70's and 80's required one to be politically correct and emphasize diversity. Being PC was not easy for me. In attempting to incorporate diversity and at the same time encourage freshman students about the value of getting a college education I thought I had a perfect illustration. I related the story of a black man by the name of Booker T. Washington who walked from his home to Hampton Institute, a distance of 400 miles.

A female student, ironically blond, raised her hand and asked, "Every day?" Thoughts raced through my mind as to how to respond without humiliating the young lady. My first thought was, "Yes, and he goes home for lunch". My thought process was going in slow motion trying to find a good answer when an older student just behind her leaned in and said, "That is like from here to Atlanta and back". Her response was, "Oh". It sounded like the light switch was still not turned to ON. That may be where we got the saying, "She is not the brightest light in the chandelier."

We learn that 'common sense' is not very common among those with less of life experiences. Some young people need to get out more. Get a job.

Home Coming – Mars Hill College

For a period of time I filmed games for the Carson Newman football team and traveled with them to away games. We were in the open press box on Homecoming day. I was filming beside the coaches and Steve Wright was chewing tobacco and spitting into a Styrofoam cup. We were not having a good game but we did have a great play on a pass that moved the ball down the field about 30 yards. Steve was so excited that he jumped up to cheer and his elbow hit his spit cup which was about half full by this time. As a movie producer the following would be in "Slow MO". The cup went flying through the air, turning and twisting toward the bleachers of the alumni of Mars Hill. The man to be on the receiving end of this 'fumble' was dressed in a pin strip suit. The up-side-down cup of brown liquid hit on his right shoulder. Steve was looking down at the man apologetically, offering to drop a clean handkerchief to him. The man was yelling something back and waving that he wanted nothing else from up there. I was then looking for a way out other than down through the bleachers that we had ascended. From the press box I could jump a 10 foot high chain link fence and land on the pavement. Not a good idea from about 30 feet up. But I wanted to be the first person on the team bus. We did manage to hide in the press box and leave without face to fact confrontation with the man in a now 'brown' pin strip suit and the smell of a desert camel. If confrontation had come, I think I would have helped the man whip Steve.

Extra Credit, Shaving points

We had the great honor of having the great nephew of the famous James Brown as a student at Carson Newman. Fuquan Warren was a football player and he was a student in one of my classes. He knew that I was a great supporter of CN athletics in general and football in particular. I had traveled with the team as

film man, what they now have is videographers. I carried the big camera and did film in a black bag and worked on top of the stadium. I loved working with the football team. It was probably a natural question for an athlete to ask, "Will Dr. Bull shave some points for an athlete." Someone asked Fuquan that question. He held up his hands with index fingers pointed upward and thumbs extended together to make the symbol of a goal post. He then pointed with his right index finger just past the left one and explained, "Dr. Bull said, 'If it goes by over here, do you get any points?'." If you have to get it through the uprights in football to get any points why should you not have to get it right to get points in class? Athletes need to learn this lesson early in their playing days and no later than middle school.

Brad's Tomato Stick Sword

When we purchased the Magna View Church parsonage there was not a single tree between our house and highway 11 E. However there was a large stand of Johnson Grass that was higher than my head. I rooted out all the Johnson grass and planted a pretty good sized garden which included tomatoes. The tomatoes were staked with some oak pieces.

Toward the end of summer while Brad was in the back yard by himself, he observed a car stop along the side of the highway behind our house. A man got out, walked around the car and slapped his female companion.

Brad was 13 or 14 years old but he ran through the garden, pulled up a tomato stake and raced over to the edge of the road. He told the man to stop bothering the lady. He did stop his action and got back into the driver's side and drove away. Brad came into the house to tell us about the valor of Sir Tomato Stick Bull.

Soon afterwards there was a knock on our front door. It was the man who had faced Sir Tomato Stick Bull and lost. He told Brad, in our hearing, that he was engaged to the young lady and they were just having a little disagreement. He assured Brad that he loved the girl and would not hit her anymore. He thanked Brad for his bravery and left.

Brad grew up to be the defender of justice and the provider of liberty for all.

The song, *God of Beauty, Truth and Goodness* was commissioned for the 150 anniversary of Carson Newman College; words by W L Forbis, music by Sandra T. Ford and Choral Arrangement by James Pethel. The second verse goes with this Tomato Stick story:

> Stand for Truth and cry for Justice, Share with those who don't belong, and remember as you serve them, sing for those who have no song. Sing a joyful alleluia, Praising God in all you do, and remember as you witness God is singing over you. (Zeph. 3:17)

Brad as a Swinger

For several years I took students from Carson Newman to do a practicum in the schools of the mountains in the area of Cosby in Cocke County. Some evenings and week-ends we did excursions into the community in the college van. On this particular day we drove up into the Cosby Campground of the Great Smoky Mountains. The Park Rangers had been doing maintenance on a hillside to restore ground cover. On the top of this hill, a good distance up, there was a large vine hanging from a tree. It was like it had a call for Tarzan to come and swing. Brad asked if he could go up and swing. His mother immediately said, "No". I stopped the van to take a look and said, "You only go around in life once. Have a swing, son."

Brad climbed up the side of the hill and over to the vine, took hold of it and with youthful vigor took a few steps backward and lunged forward. With is best adolescent Tarzan yell he released from the swinging vine and down the side of the mountain he rolled. As he slid he was breaking up the wood spikes the Park Rangers had covered with straw. At the bottom Brad looked like hamburger meat at the grocery store.

Well, I learned in teacher education that it is best when we learn by doing. Maybe he learned that in the future he should listen more to his mother. (But girls should listen to their daddy.)

Through a Child's Ears

Benita had been listening to her mother and another lady talking about a friend's pregnancy and the nearness of the delivery. One of Benita's friends was here playing and also listening to some adult talk about pregnancy. They also were discussing the expected delivery. The girl called her mom to report what she had heard but missed it a little. She gave the woman's name and then said, "She has dilated three meters." This is going to be an easy delivery! That kid will fall out.

The two girls were listening to hear Barbara on the phone saying that a certain lady could not participate in an activity because she "was tied up". Later we heard Benita on the phone telling her little friend that they needed to go to Mrs. Ray's house to untie her.

Well, she had heard that she was "tied up". So goes the literal mind of a child.

First Ultrasound

Barbara was expecting our third, and last, child. This was way different from the eighteen years ago when Brad was born. This was Jefferson Memorial Hospital. I was actually involved in the birthing process, being in the delivery room taking photos of the event. But earlier on I was involved also.

About six months into the pregnancy Barbara was going in for ultrasound and invited me to go along. On this day she had been having some rather severe, sharp pains. She would jump and grab her stomach with her hand and say "Ooooh". This continued right on into the laboratory where the technician greased her abdomen and began running that instrument round and round and watching the black and white dots on the monitor. After he heard a couple of her groans he looked at me and said, "Watch this on the monitor". I watched and saw a clump of black dots move. He looked at me, smiled and said, "The baby has hiccups."

I do not know how anyone in his/her right mind could believe this was anything other than a baby. How could anyone want to ABORT this little one?

This Father's Day 2012, Bethany and Keith announced that they are having a baby come next February. The joy continues.

Squeaky Doors on Date Night

When Brad was in high school I sometimes tried to read his assignments just to see what was in the curriculum. I remember reading Benjamin Franklin and wishing it had been on my high school reading list. All I had was the photo section of National Geographic. One day I happened upon some of Brad's creative writing. He was good even back then. This particular story was instructions on how to slip into the house after a date without disturbing your sleeping parents. It was clever as the devil. Suggestions like: park the car farther from the house so parents do not hear the car door close; if weather permits, roll the window down and come out so there is no door closing; spit on the hinges so they do not squeak, etc. All these were good suggestions.

One night Brad had a date and we stacked every pot, pan, grandma's iron skillet, and aluminum pan in the house against the front door. I do not know how many of his techniques he used that night but I do know that before he could spit on the hinges he heard the sounds of World War II reverberating through the house. No doubt he knew that we knew exactly what time he came home that night.

Remember, no matter how smart or creative you are, your parents have probably had more experience.

Bethany at the Beach

Brad was on a summer mission trip to the Philippines and Connie, his sweetheart, was doing summer missions at Myrtle Beach, South Carolina. (Now which of them do you think was smarter?) We decided that if we could not be with Brad we would be with Connie, so we planned a week trip to Myrtle Beach. There were two significant events connected to this trip.

First story: Connie's parents had just spent a week at the beach along with their other daughters. They were coming back to Knoxville as we were going to the beach. We changed our route in order for me to have a short visit with a former student. Later we stopped at a restaurant for lunch. Of all the different routes that two families could take in opposite directions, what are the chances that they would end up at the same location for lunch? Odds are enormous that it would not happen but it did. After a restroom break I looked up and saw my wife in animated conversation with what I assumed was a total stranger. This was very out of character for quiet Barbara. It was in fact not a stranger but the Cruze family. Benita asked if Cindy could go back to the beach with her for another week. They begged. Cindy's clincher was that the coincidence of our chance meeting "was the hand of God". I would not have blamed it on God but it was one chance in a million.

Bill in giving permission for Cindy to return for another week at the beach simply said, "Who am I to stand against the 'hand of God'?" Bill Cruze was one of the best men I have ever known.

On the trip to South Carolina we establish a hoax to play on Connie, the big sister who had just been left by her family. Here is the plan: Cindy is to run ahead of us to the door and excitedly tell Connie that she (Cindy) got lost from her parents and had hitch hiked back to Myrtle Beach by herself. By the time we stepped out into view, Connie was beside herself.

This brings us to the Second event which was not a planned hoax but scared us almost to death. Connie and her college friends were doing a Bible study activity on the beach. Several people had gathered around to participate. Ms B and I decided to go into the ocean for a swim and we thought we asked someone to watch Bethany. From about 100 yards out in the water Barbara screamed that she could not see Bethany. We went ashore as soon as possible to find that no one knew where Bethany was. We immediately devised a search plan while Barbara screamed that Bethany had been kid napped. Calm finally prevailed as one search party went north and one went south. A couple stayed put to wait. We wrote large messages in the sand with Bethany's name on it. A near by life guard assured us that Bethany was not in the water. He said they had never had a child under the age of five to drown because they run away from the waves. The south bound group, after about 45 minutes found Bethany being held by a life guard. He had seen her walking down the beach by herself and asked her where she was going. She said she was going to Florida. Then, as now, Bethany was always going in the right direction.

Bethany Gets a Bicycle

When Bethany was very small she had a tricycle. She rode on the front side walk and bumped into the front steps. Then she started riding the tricycle standing up. She is the only child I have ever seen do that. When she got a little older, our friend Colleen gave Bethany a scooter that her children had outgrown. She learned how to ride the scooter down the back sidewalk at a high rate of speed. I thought she was going to run into the brick wall of the side of the house. I would almost hold my breath as she raced down the side walk and at the last second veer off into the grass. She was good on wheels.

On a trip to Etowah, Bethany and I happen to go visit my brother Don. He had grandchildren by this time and one of his grandsons had outgrown his bicycle. Don said that if I did not mind Bethany having a boy's bicycle, we could have this one. It looked about her size. It needed some air in the tires so we went to the station down town and filled the tires with air and delivered the bicycle up to Grandmother Bull's house on Scott Avenue.

With family all over the back yard, I got the bicycle out of the trunk of the car, sat it on the ground. Bethany got hold of it, put her leg over, hopped up on it and rode away across the lawn. Barbara came over to me and exclaimed, "I wanted to watch you teach her how to ride". I said, "You just saw the same thing I saw". Bethany had no training wheels and no one to hold and run behind her. She just rode.

In education we talk about learning being from the simple to the complex. If you want your child to ride a bicycle, be sure he/she begins on a scooter. It is all about balance.

Bethany is about as well balanced as anyone I know.

Mr. Sun (Soon) Learns to Drive

Mr. Sun was an exchange scholar from China and he spent a good deal of time at our house, often asking for definitions for English words. He had been our guide while we taught at Yanti University in China. After he left Carson Newman he was visiting scholar at Shorter College in Georgia.

One day I received a call for a very excited Mr. Sun. The officials in China had told him that if he could get a driver's license they would provide a car for him when he returned to China. This was a really big deal for him. He wanted me to come to Georgia and teach him how to drive. No one in his right mind would ask me to teach him/her how to drive since I learned myself with a drunk man sitting beside me. (In his car) Any way I agreed to go to Georgia and teach him to drive.

I went to Shorter and picked Mr. Sun up and went to the campus of Berry College which is the largest campus in the world. It was Mr. Sun's first time to sit in the driver's seat. I talked him through the basics and we drove slowly around the wooded area of Berry College.

Suddenly he wanted to go take the driving test. I strongly urged that he was not ready but he insisted with the reason, "If I fail today, I can try again tomorrow."

At the testing station the female examiner noticed my license plate and started asking questions about the possibility of her daughter coming to college at Carson Newman. I handed my business card to her and some brief information about our college.

I left the motor running and the door open so Mr. Sun would have as little as possible to do. As I watched him drive through the test area without another car in sight I was shocked to see the windshield wipers come on since it was a perfectly beautiful day. The turn signals came on, but it was not the way he turned. Parallel parking was next and we had not practiced that. I watched in horror as the pylons were knocked over. I thought, "We are finished for today and that adds two more days to my stay in Georgia."

The tester got out of the passenger side and whispered in my ear, "We had some communication problems but he PASSED!"

Now you know why I would never drive in China and am very cautious while passing through Georgia.

20 Seconds with the First Astronaut

In 1960 Miss Jamie Huggins was my professor in English 101. It was a no-nonsense class. Her grades were C+, C- and See – me. But on this historic day of the first suborbital flight, featuring astronaut John Glenn, Miss Huggins gave permission for me to monitor my boom box. (a gift from Mavis at Powell Hardware where I worked in high school and I believe the only one on campus) I could monitor it quietly until as she put it, "Mr. Glenn is safely returned to earth."

Half listening to her lecture and wholly listening to the radio the announcer said the capsule was in the water, the hatch is off, John Glenn is lifted to the ship. I raised my hand and Miss Huggins recognized me to speak. I told her that Mr. Glenn was safely on the ship. Her response was, "Mr. Bull, you may lead us in a pray of thanksgiving for Mr. Glenn's safe return to earth." In two years of English that was the only "interruption".

Many years later our family was visiting my college classmate and his family, Dr. Kester Greene Jr, in the Baltimore area. We went for a day visit to Washington D. C. The adults and children were separated as we walked down the street when I saw a group of people preparing to play softball on the lawn. A man parked, opened the door and grabbed a softball glove from the seat. I recognized him as John Glenn, the senator from Ohio. I spoke to him and shook his hand.

Several minutes later we caught up to the rest of our group excited to tell them that we had just shook hands with America's first astronaut. They would not believe us but Brad and Benita know the truth.

I wonder if he is telling his grandchildren that he touched a teacher who touched many teachers who touched the lives of thousands of students here on the planet. I doubt it.

There is a difference between fame and value.

Watch Your Signage

While visiting an elementary school where my wife was a substitute teacher I saw a teacher coming down the hall with her class in tow. I noticed that her tee shirt had on it the word "ass" in bold letters. I stopped her and whispered in her ear that her shirt signage was inappropriate for an elementary school. She looked shocked and said, "Why?" Well it says ass. She was embarrassed and immediately removed her jacket to reveal that she had been on vacation to NASSAU, written in all capital letters.

Life is not always what the world perceives it to be. It gets better when we see the whole picture.

Skin Cancer

Delma Bull was fair skinned and red headed. In her early years she spent much time working in the sun. I remember when I was three or four years old when mom and her adoptive parents, Uncle Taylor and Aunt Hattie, were picking cotton at the New Zion farm. I was barely big enough to drag the bag and watch mom pick the cotton and see the scratches on her hands and arms.

Later I saw the skin of her face removed from her nose to her hair line and I became very conscious of staying out of the sun. By high school days I was pretty much content with being very white. There were enough days in the sun to do the damage to my skin; a few days at the beach and mowing lawns.

Not wanting to be a macho man who would not see a doctor, I went fairly regularly to the dermatologist. (Nine of ten people who die with skin cancer are men) Once there was a tiny red spot on the end of my nose and the doctor determined that it was pre-cancerous. So he took the spot off resulting in an ugly scab on the end of my nose. Something like that cannot be hidden.

I went to the book store at Carson Newman and one of the ladies who worked there asked, "What happened to your nose?" I replied, "I stuck it in someone else's business." Her quick response was, "Like I just did?"

I really had stuck my nose in the business of dermatologist, Dr. Charles Fulk. Sometimes it costs you money when you stick your nose in someone else's business. The cost in this case was better than the consequences of not spending the money

On Being Bi-Lingual in East Tennessee

Connie, my favorite daughter-in-law, took a summer job at Dollywood. She dressed in costume as a Southern Belle. Part of her employment included working in the ticket booth where you could purchase a day ticket or upgrade to a season pass.

One day she saw a family talking among themselves and eventually they sent up a little boy to purchase the tickets because he could speak a little broken English. Connie realized what was happening and told the boy, in Spanish, to go back and get his parents. When they came to the window, Connie began the transaction in fluent Spanish. One of her fellow employees turned to another employee and in a stage whisper said, "They law, she's a speakin in tongues." I suppose she thought Connie would be better suited for the little church up in the valley at Dollywood.

Dr. Connie Bull has done a fantastic job in teaching Music in the elementary school and more recently Spanish at the high school level. And she is still speaking in tongues

Development Education

One semester at Carson Newman I was assigned to teach a course in Developmental Education. The students in the class were marginally ready for college. The major weakness of these students was reading and that requires vocabulary. A major portion of the class was devoted to learning new words. I assigned 20 to 30 words per week. On the last class of the week I would give certain words and the students were required to use the word in a sentence; preferably, a sentence that made sense.

One week I gave the word, "circumscribe", circum, meaning around and scribe, meaning to write. Definition: To draw around. One of the students was an athlete, trying to stay eligible. Her sentence was: "Most Jewish males are circumscribed." I do hope she could shoot better than she could read. And I wish the early grades would do more to prepare students for the adult world. My advice to young people: Read more!

Exchange Student

Over the years we had exchange students stay in our home to broaden the cultural understanding of our own children. One such exchange student came one summer and returned to our house the next Christmas as a guest and to pick up a camera he had left in our car the previous summer. That was Tomoyuki Yabe of Tokyo, Japan.

We were returning from a trip to the Brown farm in Bristol and went through the city of Bloomingdale. Tomo could not pronounce the "bl" sound so he started practicing. He had a system of bending his knuckles to keep count of his verbal attempts. The children, mom and I were listening to this phonetic exercise until we were about crazy. I wanted to stop the car and go for a walk. My children were saying, "Daddy, make him stop". He was an international guest. What was I to do? I gently suggested that we do something else. He replied that as he bent his knuckles he was going to do it 1,000 times until he got it right.

I complimented his effort and he said something we all needed to hear. "I never grow weary of learning".

Tomo eventually returned to the U S and graduated from Syracuse University and is now a scholar of the Ethiopian language.

On a trip to the Philippines we had a stopover in Tokyo and Tomo's parents took us to a restaurant downtown. The servers met us on the street and escorted us into the business where the cook came to the table to talk with us about our order. No one else came in.

Tomo's parents had rented the entire restaurant for the evening because their home was too small to accommodate us. This was a dinner to remember for Brad, Connie, Benita and me. After dinner we went to the Tokyo Tower. What an evening to remember!

The Mullins Clan

Rev. Kelver and Mattie Mullins were Carson Newman College graduates,s were their children, grandchildren and cousins. I had their daughter in class and she relates this story about her father and maternal grandfather.

When Mattie started dating Kelver her father could never remember Kelver's name. On a date night the family was seriously trying to get the daddy to know the young suitor's name. They came up with a clever mnemonic device: "Remember the refrigerator is a Kelvinator. His name is Kelver!" They thought he had it.

That night Kelver came over for dinner. Everything was going fine until Mattie's father needed the mashed potatoes which were right in front of Kelver. After some thought he asked for the potatoes by saying, "Pass the potatoes Weston."

Well, at least he got a refrigerator and Mattie eventually got Kelver Bernard Mullins and they became one of the great Carson Newman families. Many years later Barbara and I had the great joy of accompanying Mattie on a trip to the Holy Lands of Israel.

Call in a Medical Specialist

Benita was complaining of some soreness in her throat and nothing was readily visible. After a while it seemed to get worse and I took a look as far into her throat as I could and it did seem to have something way in the back of her tongue just above the hump that goes into the throat. It looked like a boil. So we went to the Doctor. (Names here are NOT real to protect the medical persons from humiliation.) Doctor White and his nurse began the examination. Then the doctor called for a colleague, Doctor Drummer, to confirm that indeed there was something back there. Neither of them knew what it was. Finally, one of the doctors suggested that "we probe it and see what happens". He asked Benita to open wide and held her tongue with a depressor. He took another probe and reached behind the suspicious "whatever it is" thing. It popped into the front of her mouth and the doctor picked it up. Examined it and exclaimed, "It appears to be a popcorn kernel husk." Then he looked at us and said, "Please don't ever tell anyone that this happened."

It was difficult to remember how long ago Benita had eaten popped corn but that little sucker had held on while several meals and gallons of saliva had passed it by. Scientist say we should start with the most simple hypothesis. That would have helped in the popped corn dilemma.

Benita Hospitalized

We received a call in the middle of the night saying, "The children have been in a car wreck in Fort Worth." We sat in bed praying until daylight and received the rest of the message that they were in a trauma center in Fort Worth. Heath's dad and I flew out there to be with our grown children. Benita had a severe head injury with the skull bone broken. Heath's injury was not as severe and we began the weeks of visiting every day with Benita in the ICU. Her recovery was magnificent but slow.

One day as the nurse was working with Benita to check her vision, she did the typical, "How many fingers do I have up?" Benita said, "Three" but we could all see that Benita had her eyes closed. The nurse asked, "How do you know?" Benita replied, "You always start with three".

In a semi-conscious state Benita had remembered her bank account number and phone numbers of her friends. And her hearing was phenomenal. When we finally got her here to our house for recovery, we were sitting in the sun room, which in on the second floor.

Benita started complaining about all the noise. We looked at each other, wondering what noise she was talking about. She was hearing the leaves hit the ground outside. LOUD crunching noise!

We thank God that the injury had minimal long range effects. A good clear mind is important for life and especially in the life of a banker. That's BBandT!

Mrs. Jamie Hankins

Mrs. Hankins was an English teacher at Etowah High School. She was also a very dear friend of my mother and her son David was my close friend. We went to church, school, football, and everything else together for years. Mrs. Hankins was also a pipeline of information to my mother about what went on at school. Often mom knew things before I walked in the door after school.

In her latter years, Mrs. Hankins was hospitalized in the Baltimore area. Mrs. Buckner, Barbara and I went to the hospital to visit our dear friend, along with David, his wife and his sister.

We went our separate ways for the night after asking permission to leave and telling Mrs. Hankins that we would return the next morning at 10 A M. Barbara and I arrived early and were in the room when Mrs. Hankins breathed her last breath. It was exactly 10 A M.

We hurriedly made arrangements with the family to return to Tennessee and I would do the eulogy at our home church in Etowah. While I was doing the funeral arrangements Barbara worked at the Hankins house with David's wife. They were cleaning house and getting ready for receiving friends.

When I returned to the Hankins' house, I was met at the front door by David's wife and she said, "I have worked with your wife all day, and you got more than you deserved". I simply replied, "I have known David all his life, and you got exactly what you deserved."

Maybe we all get more than we deserve. Most of us are blessed. We were blessed to know Mrs. Jamie Hankins.

Civility

In Philosophy of Education class I was giving an illustration about the fact that my daddy had died before I was born. I noticed a student had big tears in her eyes. She remained after class for a discussion of her life.

She was adopted shortly after birth. Later her adoptive parents divorced and her adoptive father won custody, and later he remarried. His new wife was attractive, and a Christian who provided spiritual leadership in the new home. She became not only a step mother but a dear friend to her daughter.

Three years later this student was graduating. The ceremony was in a lighted football stadium which was beside a large unlighted sports area. After the ceremony I was exiting through that somewhat darkened area. There stood this student in tears on what should have been one of the happiest evenings of her life. I stopped to talk with her. She pointed over into the darkness and said, "Over there are my parents," She pointed in the opposite direction and said, "There is my adoptive mother, and they are not going to get any closer than that. I do not know where to go."

I believe it was in the 1960's when there was a White House conference to define "family". My opinion is that however you define "family", there should be civility at times of ceremony. We should ask ourselves, "For what person or persons is this event being held?" Then we need to do whatever it takes to make the event special for the person/persons. For graduations, weddings, funerals, etc. let us be civil.

The student in the story above remains a dear friend with whom we visit at home coming events. She is raising a family that is beautiful and close, like all children should have. Civility comes with love, spite comes with selfishness.

Mission Trips

The Beijing China X ray Machine

We were leading a team of teachers to teach Chinese middle and secondary teachers how to speak East Tennessee English, which was the only kind we could speak. We were going through the old airport and a piece of luggage became lodged inside the big metal box on the conveyer belt. The entrance to the box was covered with large strips of clear plastic. From our up front position we could not see the larger than life monitor on top of the machine but the team behind us could see it clearly.

Ms. B, always the servant helper, not wanting to be held up, reached through the plastic strips to move the luggage and get the conveyer belt moving again. Suddenly we heard some men behind us saying, "Great lungs Ms B". They were all watching a live breast examination. X rays have greatly improved since then but just last week returning from South Africa we were in the London airport and I said, "B, if the luggage gets stuck, do not help".

Bethany's Cheeseburger

We were on the way to Yanti University in China to teach Oral English to high school and middle school teachers of English. The trip involved a two day layover in Hong Kong. The city was exciting to visit and we knew that evening that it would be our last chance to eat at McDonald's. This restaurant was the largest any of us had ever seen. Imagine a McDonald's that is two stories high and every line has 20-30 people in it. And everyone is in a hurry.

Bethany was eight years old. As she placed her order, to an employee who was NOT bi-lingual, she asked for a "Cheeseburger, with No mayonnaise." We received our orders and went to the second floor looking for a place to be seated. Finally we found a table for four. Bethany opened her sandwich. I do mean opened it up to see that she had two pieces of bread and a slice of cheese. This was a Hong Kong Cheeseburger from a waiter who could hear only the beginning consonant in Mayonnaise which is the same sound in the beginning of Meat. Double cheeseburger, no meat! I believe we would call that an American cheese sandwich.

The place was way too busy to go back through the line to correct the order but Bethany's mom had a real double cheeseburger and shared a slice of meat.

Bethany became the favorite teacher of the Chinese students. She taught them how to play Uno. Because she was a very young lady, they were not afraid to talk with her.

"I'm playing a Red Reverse!" They had to use whole sentences, moving toward, "Give me a double cheeseburger with no mayonnaise."

Honduran Chic'le (chewing gum)

On a return from a mission trip it was customary to be asked to give a report about the work of the medical/dental team to our local congregation. We were always looking for something to bring home that would be of particular interest to the children at our church. Some time we would purchase vanilla or coffee to share with the adults. It was also our practice to barter with the vendors in Honduras. On one occasion I saw some chic 'le and wanted to obtain the entire case. After some up and down bartering I felt really good about my success at getting this chewing gum for our children back home. The case had those tiny boxes that contain two pieces of gum.

After our presentation of slides at our church and talking about the work in Honduras, I began handing out little boxes of chewing gum to the children. I told them it was chic'le as a gift from

Honduras. Shortly a small boy came up to me, pointed to the edge of the tiny box where he said was printed, "Made in New Jersey".

Okay, my eye sight is not as good as it once was but is it not "the thought that counts"? Was it Honduran chic`le if it was purchased in Honduras?

Hobo at Church

Ms B and I had the great opportunity to teach English as a Second Language at Yanti University in China. A church up in Virginia was having a mission conference and someway the pastor heard about us and invited me to come up there as a guest speaker. This place was 130 miles away from our house so I was unknown to the people up there. The pastor and I conferred about my plan for the evening and he went along with it.

Arriving at the church, dressed as a transient and pretending to be a deaf mute, I carried a very old, small, blue suitcase. The church members had prepared a covered dish meal that covered about six tables. A real spread.

I wrote on a scrap paper that I was hungry and homeless. The person called for the head deacon. He explained by writing and by motions that they would put me up in a motel for one night and I could eat a meal at the motel restaurant. I signaled to him that I wanted to eat here at their table. He reluctantly pointed for me to get in the line.

After fixing my plate and being seated I got out chopsticks and began eating. A lady seated near me asked how I had learned to eat with chopsticks. I wrote down, "Hunan's"

The use of chopsticks at a mission conference should have been a harbinger for the lady to suspect something but it didn't.

When it came time for the program the pastor said, "Dr. Bull has not arrived to do the program". I raised my hand and

SAID, "I'm right here". I opened the suit case and began to tell them about my work in China. I do believe the head deacon and the lady seated near me nearly died of shock.

Fifteen years later my next door neighbor, Dr. Kester Greene Jr, was working up in Virginia as school superintendent. There was a man in his community who told him about a Hobo that came to speak at his church. Kester came home that week-end and asked if that had been my story. He thought he remembered hearing it before.

Two things to learn here: The element of surprise is a great teaching technique and you never know when you might be entertaining angels unaware. Be kind to Hobos.

The Grandchildren

Delyn is Obedient (Reluctantly)

She was big enough to walk and talk and strong willed. One day at our house she took some food and beverage from the table and started walking toward the den. I told her to stop and she could not take the food into the den. She took the next defiant step and I said, "Delyn, if you go in there I will bust your butt". She looked over her shoulder and said, "Time Out". My response to her was, "Grandpop has no idea what time out means but I will bust your butt if you go in there". She turned and came back to the table to eat and drink.

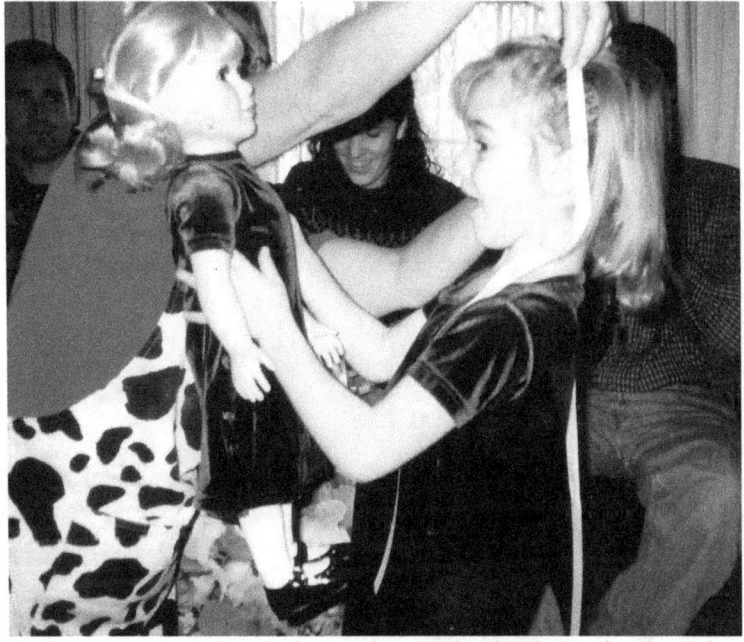

A few years later her little brother had joined the family. John-

Clarke was here with her and he was playing behind the curtains at the sliding door. I asked him to stop playing with the curtains. He could just barely walk but he could pull hard. I walked in the kitchen and heard Delyn as she went over to little brother and said, "Grandpop can bust your butt."

    I still do not know if Time Out works but I know we have two wonderful grandchildren.

The Outhouse

John-Clarke had grown to four or five years of age when they were on a trip to the Spring House in McMinn County. Early on we had decided to keep the place primitive so the grandchildren and their cousins could see how our grandparents lived in rural East Tennessee. Therefore we had an outdoor fire pit for boiling water and cooking, cool drinks down in the spring water, and Tony had built an outhouse. (A one holer) This was the first time that John Clarke had gone in to relieve himself in the outhouse. He came out and said to Delyn, "How do you flush that thing?"

Now that everything is supposed to be "green" I don't see the environmentalists rushing to build outhouses that use NO water. Sprinkle a little lime in the hole and the smell is gone and you waste no water. Go GREEN!

Delyn's Dessert

Delyn was about four or five years old when visiting us at meal time. She always liked our pancakes with all the side dressings. One of her delights was Dream Whip. On this day the Dream Whip container was almost empty and she had spooned out most of it and looked like she wanted more but it was hardly worth all the work with the spoon. So, I suggested that she take her hand, reach down in the container, run it around and around and then lick it off her fingers. After a few seconds of looking at me in amazement as if to say, "Can I believe that my Grandpop really suggested that?" Then in childlike wisdom she proclaimed, "I don't think that is a very good idea."

That is called reverse psychology. It works great with four year olds and college students who think they are ready for marriage. Go for it! Lick your chops.

John-Clarke and Today's Technology

John-Clarke from birth has not been a great housekeeper of his room. At times I have tried to assist in encouraging him to be neat. Everything has a place and should be in its place. On one occasion I was helping with cleaning his room. I picked up a shoe that looked like it had much wear left in it and asked him, "Where is the other shoe?" He replied that it did not matter. Well, it did matter because I was putting things in their proper place. Looking at the perfectly fine treaded shoe I asked again, "John-Clarke, where is the other shoe?" In his final disgust with my persistence

he declared, "It does not matter Grandpop, they don't light up any more."

Thinking of the times as a child I put cardboard inside my shoes to cover the holes that had worn in the bottom, I was grateful that my grandson would not have to experience that level of poverty. I am glad that he has shoes that light up. But what lights my heart up more is that he is learning to use what he has to help the less fortunate.

The Mosquito Spray

We had heard or read somewhere that a good way to keep mosquitoes away was to spray Listerine in the area. So we purchased a clear plastic spray bottle and filled it about half way full of green Listerine. We found that it did work and so left the container on the porch to use in the evening down at the spring house.

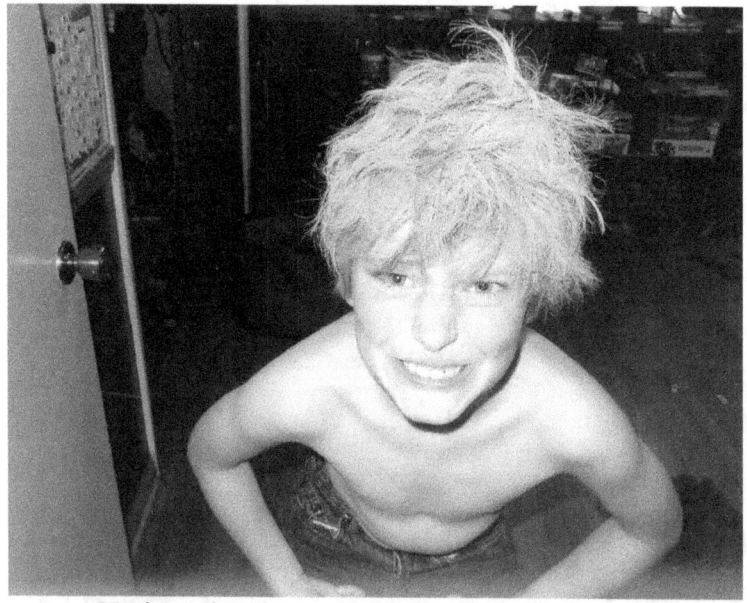

Having privately coached John-Clarke we set out to have some practical joke fun. As the family was gathered on the porch in chairs and swings, we were watching the sun go down and hearing the birds sing. (As evening falls there may be mosquitoes.) In a pretty loud voice I requested that John-Clarke spray for mosquitoes. He picked up the green Listerine and began spraying it all around. Then he turned the spray toward his mouth and said, "Watch this". As the first squirt hit his mouth both his mother and father were on their feet headed toward him and yelling in one of those slow motion things you see in movies, Noooooooooooooooooooooooo! Son!

As he spit out that batch he said, "It's just Listerine". Everyone had a great laugh, well not everyone. Brad and Connie had not yet gotten their breath back.

I love to see my grandchildren playfully make their parents "rise up". It pays them back for all the times they made their parents "rise up".

Long Legs

It was reported as research on a national news network concerning the attractiveness of women: Men like women with long legs. If you have two women of the same height but one of them has longer legs, men will be more attracted to that one. (Photo example)

If you are given to watching Attractiveness Pageants on television you could verify this research for yourself. I know

empirically that the research is true.

One day my daughter-in-law and granddaughter were at our dining room table and I related the research to my granddaughter, Delyn by way of telling her that men were going to find her attractive because she was blessed with long legs. She returned to the table from the refrigerator. Then I said to her, "Do you know what women find attractive about men?" (This is NOT research and the longer my sentence gets the larger Delyn's mom's eyes get.) Delyn said, "No, what do women find attractive about men".

My response: "The size of their ………wallet."

Oh, they claim it is all about LOVE but it probably matters some that he has potential for financial success.

There is a song, "You'll Always be Beautiful in My Eyes." That song emphasizes that attractiveness may fade but BEAUTY is an inner quality that grows with age. I have found that true in the life of my wife of 50 years, who is more and more beautiful and she has great legs.

The Promise

Keeping My Word

In August of 1960 I was on the sidewalk in front of Henderson Humanities Building at Carson Newman College. It was freshman orientation day. Just in front of me was a cute girl with a yellow ribbon in her hair. I started a conversation with her and asked about her plans for life. She replied that she wanted to be a missionary to Africa. I said to her, "I would like to go to Africa with you".

As we talked I asked if I could look at her class ring. (The Bluff City Grizzlies) As the professor called us into the building I slipped her class ring into my pocket, insuring that she would find me and indeed she did. The next day, as I sat in the cafeteria with some guys, she approached me with a rather loud, "I want my ring back". Well, the guys thought we were breaking up. That is how she got her name on the list of five girls I had decided I wanted to date. On December 28 of our junior year we married at Euclid Avenue Baptist Church in Bristol, Virginia. This was also the anniversary of her parents wedding.

After college we would work in several countries in short term mission work including China, Russia and Honduras. But we made no trips to Africa.

Today, as I write this, we are sitting in a Chicago airport waiting for a flight to London and Cape Town, South Africa. This trip is in celebration of our 50th wedding anniversary. I said, "I would like to take you to Africa", fifty-two years ago and now I am fulfilling that wish. I keep my word.

The Conclusion and Post Script

Conclusion

Now I am beginning to listen to some of their stories for the second or third time. I rarely have the nerve to say, "Son, you have told me this before." Being a grandparent and retired gives you more time to listen and the ability to pretend that you are hearing it for the first time. But it is harder to laugh as hard the second time as I did the first time.

Now remind me about the big fish you caught.

Post Script

When, or if, my children and grandchildren visit me in the nursing home (LORD willing) they will not have to say, "Dad, (Grandpop) you have already told this story," they can just say, "Page____." Now, remind me, what was it about the big fish you caught?

Contact Information

Bernard F. Bull
1141 East Old A J Highway
Talbott, TN 37877
bbull@cn.edu
(865) 475-4815

www.ingramcontent.com/pod-product-compliance
Lightning Source LLC
Chambersburg PA
CBHW050201130526
44591CB00034B/1685